LIVING IN THE NOW

How to Live as the Spiritual Being
That You Are

D0863283

LIVING IN THE NOW

How to Live as the Spiritual Being
That You Are

Gina Lake

Endless Satsang Foundation

GRAND ISLAND PUBLIC LIBRARY

Endless Satsang Foundation

www.radicalhappiness.com

Cover art: © Emelisa Mudle
www.emelisahealingarts.com

ISBN: 978-1456472115

Copyright © 2010 by Gina Lake

All rights reserved. No part of this book may be used or reproduced by any means, graphic, electronic, or mechanical, including photocopying, recording, taping, or by any information storage retrieval system without the written permission of the publisher except in the case of brief quotations embodied in critical articles and reviews.

09 12

CONTENTS

INTRODUCTION

My hope is that the short essays in this book will help you become more conscious of your true nature and that they will provide you with the practical wisdom you need to live in this world as the spiritual being that you are. They can be read in any order and used in daily contemplation. May they serve to bring you into the greater Wholeness.

A Note About Terms

The terms I've used in this book and my others are very similar to those that Eckhart Tolle, bestselling author and spiritual teacher, has used in his books, *The Power of Now* and *A New Earth.* In those books, he introduced the term *the Now* to refer to the present moment. He also introduced the term *egoic mind,* which is the aspect of the mind that serves the ego, or the false self. *The ego* is the sense of being a *me* and all the ideas, beliefs, and other conditioning entailed in the sense of existing as an individual. The ego is called the false self because the ego isn't who we really are, although it seems that this is who we are.

The egoic mind, which is a reflection of the ego and its conditioning, is the chatterbox mind, which produces a nearly constant flow of commentary about life based on our conditioning. We experience it as "the voice in the head," as Eckhart Tolle calls it. For simplicity, I sometimes refer to the egoic mind as *the mind.* However, the egoic mind is distinct from *the functional mind,* which is the aspect of the mind that we use to read, calculate, analyze, design, follow instructions, and so forth. We need the functional mind, but we don't actually need the egoic mind to function.

In writing about the ego, I have somewhat positioned it as the enemy, as a device to help people detach from it. When people are identified with the ego, they are, in a sense, in love with the egoic mind, and I'm hoping to help them fall out of love with it, because the ego and the thoughts and feelings it produces are the source of human suffering. Of course, even the ego belongs to the Oneness, and the ego serves exactly the function the Oneness intended.

The ego isn't actually an entity. Rather, it is the *sense* of being a separate individual, which is innate to us. We feel like individuals, although we are actually manifestations, or expressions, of One Being. This is the Oneness that mystics throughout time have realized as being behind all life and which the term *non-dual*, which means "not two," refers to. While cloaked in a human body, we have lost awareness of our true nature, and we are meant to rediscover the truth. That discovery is what the spiritual path is all about and what spiritual practices are meant to reveal.

The sense of being a separate individual is accomplished through the mind. We are programmed to *think* of ourselves as separate and as having distinct characteristics and labels: "I'm a man," "I'm smart," "I'm a mother," "I'm forty-seven." Anything that comes after "I am," defines us, and we take those definitions as who we are. And yet when you examine those assumptions, you see that they are just ideas. There is no *you* behind the thoughts about you. This *you* that you think you are is made up of thoughts! What a revelation that is!

Then who are you? That is the perennial question. Trying to answer it results in the discovery that we are not a *thing*, but more of a being, an experience of existing. If we strip away all labels and ideas, we are left with just *I am*, just existence. We are that which is existing right here and now and aware of that existence. Spiritual teachers often call the true self *Awareness* because the experience of the true self is that it is aware. Beyond that, who or what we really are can't be defined. It has qualities that can be felt, such as peace, acceptance, love, compassion, gratitude, kindness, patience, wisdom, and strength, although those words don't come close to defining the mystery of our true nature.

Who we really are is indescribable because it is beyond anything the mind can grasp. But to speak about who we really are, we have to give it a name. It has been given many names: the Source, Spirit, Oneness, Beingness, Consciousness, God, Awareness, the Divine, the Absolute, Presence, Stillness, Emptiness, the Now, Essence, the Self, the higher self, the essential self, and the true self, to name just a few. I usually refer to it as Essence, the Oneness, the Self, or Awareness. Those words mean basically the same thing. I generally use *Essence* to refer to the aspect of the Oneness that expresses itself and lives through each of us. Words and definitions aren't important. You know Essence when you experience it, just as you know the ego when you experience it. Essence and the ego feel very different and are very distinct.

Awakening is another term that may need some definition. Humanity as a whole is awakening out of the egoic state of consciousness into awareness of its true nature. Many of you are taking that step. Awakening refers to the shift from identification with the ego, or false self, to the recognition of yourself as the spiritual being that you are. This shift happens whenever we are simply in the moment without all of our thoughts. So awakeness is possible in any moment. Awakening, however, generally implies a more permanent shift to living from a place of non-identification with the ego and alignment with our true nature.

1: JUST THIS

It all boils down to *now,* this moment. The experience you are having right now is it. The present moment is life—it's what is real. And the moment is just what it is. You can pile all the thoughts, feelings, and imaginations you want into this moment, but this moment is still just this. And no matter how much or how little money you have, how youthful or old you are, how talented or untalented you are, how successful or unsuccessful you are, you still have just this moment. No billionaire has any more or less of this moment. People try to dress this moment up in ideas, but it still comes down to just this simple moment. You can love it or hate it, but you still just have this moment.

As you read this, just notice the experience of being in the moment. What do you notice? What makes up this particular moment? What sounds? Sensations? Inner experiences or sensing? Sights? Also notice what thoughts and feelings might be here, but just notice them and then return to noticing everything else that's part of the moment: your body against the chair, your eyes reading these words, the sensations that are part of being alive, the ability to witness and experience the moment through the body-mind. What a miracle! This is it. Experience. Pure and simple. Everyone has the same access to experience. What we own or do or think makes no difference in our ability to experience life. Experience is an equal opportunity employer. Everyone gets the same amount of experience. We don't even need all of our senses to be working to experience life. We just need to be alive.

The ego is always trying to improve on the present moment, but instead, it ruins it with its dissatisfaction. It tells us the present moment would be better *if*: "if I had more money," "if I were in a relationship," "if I were thinner," "if I were better looking," "if I lived somewhere else," "if that hadn't happened," "if I hadn't...," "if I had...," and on and on. Those are all lies. None of those things change your experience of the moment unless you believe they do. If you believe you need anything else to be happy, you won't enjoy the moment. You won't really let yourself fully experience it. If you don't believe you need anything more to be happy than what's here right now, you discover you have everything you need.

You don't need anything more than the experience you are having right now. It's enough. It's plenty. It's perfect just as it is. It was designed for you, given to you. All you have to do, and all you have ever had to do is accept this gift. Take it and let it in. Let yourself experience the present moment just as it is. It doesn't get any better than this. That is the simple truth the ego refuses to accept, and it will suffer as long as that is the case.

No amount of spiritual seeking will ever make a difference unless you accept this simple fact: This is it. Seeking promises much more—the constant bliss the ego is after, which will never be, not in this dimension. This isn't bad news, but really good news. It's bad news to the ego because the ego is convinced that the present moment isn't good enough and that it can't be happy *yet*. But it's very good news for the *you* who is waking up out of the ego: There's something else here besides the ego's striving and dissatisfaction.

Peace and happiness are right here, right now for everyone—anyone, that is, who is willing to ignore the ego's dreams of glory, success, and unending happiness and pleasure. The ego's dreams are just that, and they keep us from being present to life just as it is and discovering what a gift it is just as it is.

The ego can get really angry when confronted with the truth. It doesn't want life to be the way it is! That is the perennial problem and why people suffer so—they take on the ego's point of view. But if you just let yourself drop out of the egoic mind and into the experience you are having right here, right now, you can discover a quiet peace and contentment that's beyond the ego, which can be your ongoing experience of life.

This that you are is always content. When you aren't paying attention to the ego's dreams, desires, and discontentment, there is an opportunity to discover what's content with this life. That is the real you. You are meant to be happy, not because you have attained or achieved something, but because it's possible to experience the ever-present happiness of your true self. It has always been possible for you to be happy; it's only a matter of discovering who or what is always happy.

2: WHY BAD THINGS HAPPEN

It would be more accurate to say "things happen" than "bad things happen." There's a world of difference between those two statements. The first one is true, and the second one is a story told by the ego. "Bad," after all, is a concept; it doesn't exist. We can't touch it, hear it, see it, or even sense it in any way. "Bad" is an idea that egos can generally agree on, but that doesn't make that concept true or real. That's the problem with consensus reality: What's accepted as true often isn't, but seeing things otherwise can be challenging.

There's hardly anything more pervasive in consensus reality than the concept of good/bad. It is the ego's primary judgment—something is either good or bad, usually in relationship to *me*. That is how the ego sees the world. The fact that everyone else who is ego identified also sees the world this way doesn't make it true. So when people ask why bad things happen, it's a trick question. It presumes bad things are happening and, in truth, they aren't—*things* are happening.

What underlies the question of why bad things happen is the belief that bad things shouldn't happen or, more truthfully, that "things I don't like shouldn't happen to me," which is an egocentric point of view. Things happen, and they happen to everyone. What the ego is really concerned about is not that bad things happen to other people, but that bad things happen to *me* and those close to *me*. It's a rare individual who suffers over bad things happening to others, and those who do so are probably too busy serving others to be suffering themselves.

"Bad things happening to me" is a problem for the ego, and it's angry about it. "Bad things happening" ruins its plans, its goals, its dreams, its self-image, its idea of invincibility. Bad things happening is definitely a problem for the ego, which would like to pretend it has life under control, even if other people don't. "Bad things happening to me" is the ego's nemesis because it lays bare the truth: The ego isn't all powerful and able to make life go as it would like. This is very bad news for the ego, perhaps even worse than the "bad" thing that happened.

What isn't seen by the ego is that its very judgment of good and bad creates the suffering, not actual circumstances or events. Many have discovered this secret in the midst of difficult circumstances. They have seen that their attitude and perspective make all the difference in how they manage during challenging times. There is no doubt that life can be very difficult, uncomfortable, painful, exhausting, lonely, frightening, or sad. However, life is never bad, which would imply that life is inherently flawed or evil. Challenging circumstances and events aren't evil or a mistake, but just part of life. They even serve a purpose in making us stronger and wiser and bringing us back in touch with our true nature. But even if challenges didn't do that, this is just the way it is. Difficulties are neither punishment nor a means of persecuting us. They aren't personal.

Everyone has his or her share of unpleasant and challenging circumstances, and over all of our lifetimes, everyone's share is about the same. However, some people manage challenges better than others, and that is what is in our hands. While we may have no choice about what happens to us, we do have a choice about how we respond to it. We can respond in ways that cause others and ourselves more suffering or in ways that don't. We can learn from our trials or not. It's up to us. Some choices yield much better results than others. Most of the suffering on earth is caused by egos hurting others and themselves by making unwise choices. The rest of the suffering is caused by egos responding negatively to the challenges of life.

The ego causes suffering and the experience of "this is bad." Without that story, life just is the way it is. People are the way they are. They do what they do. Illness happens, aging happens, death happens, destruction happens, mistakes happen, loss happens. These experiences are part of life. Without these challenges, life on earth wouldn't be life on earth, but some other experience. This is the way it is here.

Accepting that this is the way life is for everyone, not just you, is the way out of suffering. Accepting life just as it is and then doing the best you can with it, making the most loving choice in every moment, will turn a so-called bad event into a fruitful one. We all are master alchemists—we have the power to transform our experience of life by how we respond to the things we can't change. There is much about life we can't change, but when we respond with love and kindness, miracles happen: "Bad" things become good. We can learn to see life from the perspective of the Oneness, which has created all of it and sees it all as good. And so it is.

3: THE EGO VS. ESSENCE

Goodness is inherent in humanity, but it's covered over by the ego, which most people are identified with. People at their core are good and want to be good, but the ego drives them with fear to do things that harm themselves and others. The ego also uses judgments to separate itself from others, make itself superior, feel right, and pretend it knows, when knowing isn't possible. The ego is the source of all suffering, not circumstances, for it's always possible to feel the peace, contentment, and love of Essence no matter what is being experienced because those feeling-states represent our true nature, and our true nature is always present.

Essence is alive and living each of us, and it feels loving, peaceful, and content toward life in every moment. When we drop into Essence, we feel that as well. It's always possible to touch into Essence, but the egoic mind makes it difficult. It tells us life is terrible and shouldn't be the way it is. It tells us life is scary, it's dangerous, and it's cruel. The ego's advice comes from fear and its misperceptions about life and is, therefore, highly untrustworthy. The ego isn't wise because it doesn't see life truly. It sees life negatively, and that is the opposite of the truth. Life is good, and it's possible in any moment to experience the wonder, awe, joy, and respect Essence has for life instead of the disdain and fear the ego feels.

Humanity is waking up out of the ego. As part of this process, we come to see there are two possibilities: paying attention to the egoic mind or tuning into Essence. The ego was created to provide the challenges and growth that Essence enjoys. The ego creates the messes and the pain, which are experiences Essence embraces and is willing to have. And yet, there comes a time when we are ready to be done with our suffering and wake up to the truth of who we are. Since you are reading this, it must be time to see that. It's time to see that you are not the ego, although you have one. You are what has created it all and what is now manifesting as one aspect of that creation. What a blessing and what an amazing thing it is to discover that!

4: ACCEPT THE EGO

We are programmed to identify with the ego and believe the thoughts that appear in our mind that come from the ego. Following this false self is like following a false master. Realizing this now can only improve your life. Just because most people don't realize that the egoic mind is unhelpful, useless, and untrue doesn't change this fact.

Once we have begun to see this, there's often a tendency to go to battle with the voice in our head—to argue with it, tell it to go away, and feel angry or upset by it. That reaction is actually a reaction on the part of the ego to its own discovery. The ego takes control once again by resisting and fighting itself, which is how the ego deals with life in general. Going to battle with the egoic mind is just more ego. When we do that, we still aren't at peace with life or ourselves.

When we have truly stepped outside of the ego, there's nothing but acceptance, even of the egoic mind. After all, what we truly are has created everything, including the illusion that we are this limited self, so it must also be accepting the ego. Once you see the truth about the egoic mind, the appropriate relationship to it is one of acceptance, which is the relationship Essence has to it. You accept the egoic mind as a natural part of being human.

With that acceptance comes the power to choose to identify with our thoughts or not. Acceptance is a place of choice, while rejecting our thoughts or going to battle with them only keeps us involved with them. You accept that the egoic mind and its negativity are part of being human. You accept and understand that such thoughts are untrue and unnecessary and that the mind's negativity doesn't define you. Once you really see this, the egoic mind loses its power over you, the power to cause you to identify with it.

When we are identified with the egoic mind, we are following it, believing it, and loving it, unquestioningly. When we are accepting it, we are outside of it and seeing the truth about it and not giving our attention to it. Accept that this false self exists within you and all of humanity, but give your attention, love, and allegiance to something else. Love the truth.

Like all villains, the ego is a foil: It shows us, through contrast, what truth and goodness are. In this world, the Dark and the false help us know the Light and the Truth. So in the end, the villain is simply what drives this adventure of life from the Dark to the Light, and the ego fulfills that purpose perfectly.

5: THOUGHTS ARE VERY CONVINCING

Thoughts are designed to be very convincing. As soon as we think a thought, we believe it. We have to learn to stand apart from and question our thoughts before it becomes clear how few of them are actually true. "I'm not pretty," "He shouldn't have left," "I can't do that," "I can't take any more rejection," "She doesn't care"—such thoughts are *felt* to be true, and so they are believed and therefore spoken convincingly, as if they were true. And because we are convinced when we speak them, others become convinced as well.

The funny thing, though, is that being convinced of something doesn't make it so. Con artists and salesmen convince people all the time of things that aren't true because they know how to sound believable. The best salesmen are the ones who believe in their product, but a salesman can be just as effective by *pretending* to believe in a product. If that person is so convinced, then, we are likely to be convinced too. But believing something doesn't make it so. Many contestants on the TV show "American Idol" believe they are going to win, but only one actually wins.

However, in the world of the ego, believing makes it so. Believing is how the ego creates its reality. Its reality is based on beliefs and ideas, not necessarily on what's real and true. Our beliefs create our mental reality (not necessarily reality itself). For the ego to create a mental reality, thoughts have to be believable. If thoughts weren't felt to be believable, then the ego's mental reality couldn't be sustained. So part of having an ego is having thoughts that are felt to be believable, no matter how untrue they are. Even when our thoughts contradict each other, they can still seem believable, unless we consciously question them. Once we see how untrue our thoughts actually are, the ego's mental reality begins to fall apart. It can only be sustained by believing that our thoughts are true.

Something we believe to be true that isn't is called a *delusion*, and people who believe something that isn't true are said to be *deluded* or *delusional*. That would describe most of humanity, since most people are deeply identified with their egoic mind, the voice in their head, and its mistaken ideas and limiting beliefs. When we believe that voice, we are deluded. The mental world created by the ego is a delusional world. That is why spiritual teachers often refer to the world as an illusion. The world, itself, isn't an illusion, but the mental world created by the ego is. The world experienced through the lens of the ego is an illusion.

Waking up out of the ego's illusory world requires seeing that no matter how convincing our thoughts are, they are mostly untrue. And the same goes for feelings, which make our thoughts even more convincing. For instance, when you feel sad because you believe something (a story the egoic mind is telling), that makes the thought that caused you to feel sad all the more believable. Thoughts create feelings, which are felt physically, and then those physical sensations lend credibility to the original thought, which had no truth or basis in reality. Brilliant! Who thought this up? Well, the Oneness is pretty clever!

Yes, thoughts are very convincing. The ego is the penultimate con artist, and we are meant to catch the ego at its game. Once we have seen the truth, we can't be fooled anymore. We are too wise to keep falling for the same tricks, except maybe occasionally! The ego is tricky, and it gets trickier the wiser we get. It doesn't fully disappear, and it doesn't have to as long as we continue to remember that all thoughts about *me* are false, every last one of them. They tell a story about the false self, and there's no one here that those stories are true of.

Who you really are can't be described in words and has no past or future. Who you really are is the consciousness that's looking out of your eyes and experiencing the words on this page. You are just This: nameless, formless, empty nothingness and everythingness, pretending to be you for the time being. And the way it pretends to be you is by making your thoughts believable. That is how the false self—the *you* that you think of yourself as—is created. That's fine, until it's time to wake up and see what's really going on.

6: LOVE THE EXPERIENCE YOU ARE HAVING

If the experience you are having is the right experience—and it is—then you might as well love it. It makes no sense to do anything else. It's the only thing you've got! You don't have any other experience but this one right now. The ego pretends that another experience is possible, but it isn't. That is the core lie. The egoic mind affects the experience you are having, coloring it with its stories, images, fears, desires, and perceptions, but you are still only having *this* experience.

When we choose to love the experience we are having, we actually do fall in love with it. We feel happy. How do you love an experience you don't like? That may seem impossible, but loving something is only a matter of giving it our attention. You can always do that, can't you? Whatever we give our attention to is what we are loving. Love flows to whatever we give our attention to: If you are giving attention to what is going on in the moment, you are loving the moment. If you are giving attention to negative thoughts, you are loving those thoughts (you are saying yes to them), and you remain in the ego's realm.

First comes attention, then comes love. So give your attention to what's going on *outside* the egoic mind—to real life. Give it to what's true and real—to what you are sensing and experiencing, to what you are doing, or to just being. In any moment, thoughts might be part of that potpourri, but if we don't give our attention to those thoughts exclusively, which tend to be about the *me*, other people, the past or the future, they'll remain in the background and be experienced as insignificant. As soon as we give our attention to those thoughts, however, they suddenly loom large and fill the space. Everything else stops being noticed and experienced. This wouldn't be such a problem if such thoughts weren't the cause of so much suffering.

Being absorbed in thoughts about *me,* other people, the past, and the future creates so much unnecessary unhappiness. But being in the moment, with those thoughts in the background, is very pleasant and peaceful. When we are present to life as it is showing up, we experience a wonderful curiosity, excitement, and *joie de vivre* that flow from just being, because who we really are feels that way about life. That joy and wonderment are always available simply by paying attention to what our Being is up to. Our Being, Essence, is having a good time, no matter what's happening because it finds it all so precious and interesting.

When you really choose to have the experience you are having, you discover the rightness and preciousness of it. Nothing needs to be changed about it. Besides, whatever is happening is already changing into something else. The present moment is rare—there is no other moment like it. That alone makes it worth giving our attention to. Give the present moment your attention, and the love will follow. But give your attention to egoic thoughts, and the false self is born, and along with it, suffering.

7: AN EXERCISE FOR BEING IN THE NOW

Here's a simple exercise that can bring you into the Now, and you can do it anywhere and anytime.

Look at your hands. They are a marvel aren't they? Notice how they move without even thinking about moving them. Notice how they feel. Notice any warmth. Notice any tingling. That warmth and tingling is life energy. There is a subtle energy that enlivens your hands and the rest of your body, which moves through and surrounds your body and brings life to what would be just flesh.

Your hands are alive, and that aliveness can be felt. Take a moment and just feel that aliveness. It's experienced subtly, like a vibration, tingling, or warmth. Notice how that aliveness is not only in your hands, but also throughout your body. Can you feel it in your face? Your scalp? Your feet? Your arms? Your thighs? Your chest? Every part of your body is alive, and that aliveness can be felt subtly by you when you pay attention to it. Paying attention to the aliveness automatically brings you into the Now. Experiencing life brings us into life and brings us to life, you could say.

Now notice what's aware of your hands and the aliveness in your hands. What is looking out of your eyes and noticing? What is noticing is not what thinks. Noticing is separate from thinking. Noticing is silent, allowing, receptive, gentle, non-evaluative, and simply experiencing whatever is being noticed. When you are noticing, you may also experience some rejoicing in that noticing, since being aware of life is essentially a joyous experience. What a miracle it is to be alive, aware, and to have a vehicle for experiencing life! Without the body you have and without the consciousness that is connected to that body, you couldn't have even the simplest experience.

What is aware and gazing out of your eyes, marveling at your hands and at all of life, is who you really are. Who you really are is not a thing but Awareness of all things, all experience, all thought, all feelings. This that you are is totally in love with life and with everything it is aware of. It doesn't judge experience as good or bad, but says yes to all of it.

Notice how the voice in your head is just one aspect of experience. The Awareness that you are experiences the voice in your head. Thoughts are one more thing that arises in the spaciousness that is Awareness. The Awareness allows and accepts the egoic mind, just as it allows and accepts everything else. Once you have realized that you are this Awareness, life becomes wondrous, free, and joyful. All the striving to get somewhere and the sense of never having or being enough are just *ideas* that the ego has about life, nothing but ideas. It's okay for those ideas to exist, but once you recognize what is really living your life, you don't believe them anymore.

8: NOTICING LIFE

We are always paying attention to something. Most people give most of their attention to what they are thinking and only a little to what is going on around them. Usually, what they perceive and experience is highly colored by what they are thinking, like seeing the world through a pair of glasses colored by beliefs, ideas, desires, fears, dreams, preferences, memories, and opinions. Such thoughts don't help us function more effectively in the world. At best, they don't interfere too much; at worst, they drain our energy and efficiency, slant our perceptions, and interfere with tapping into the wisdom within us that is available in every moment.

The egoic mind pretends to be wise and have answers, but the mind isn't where wisdom comes from. Wisdom isn't a thought or belief. Wisdom may draw on information, but information alone doesn't result in wisdom. If you examine the egoic mind, you discover that much of what this voice in your head tells you is just plain false, and the rest is useless. That voice takes a position and holds it because that opinion is *its* opinion, not necessarily because that position has been carefully examined. It's amazing how quickly people jump to conclusions and form an opinion, just to have one. And once they have one, they are convinced of their viewpoint: "It's my opinion, so it must be right!"

The commentator in your head is not you. It's especially not a wise *you*. Would you listen to this voice if it weren't going on in your head? We can use our functional, rational mind to see through this more primitive aspect of the mind, which has taken control and pretends to be us but doesn't deserve control. It doesn't deserve our attention.

The worst thing about giving our attention to this voice in our head is that if we are involved with it, we can't give our attention to something else that is truer and more fulfilling. We can only attend fully to one thing at a time. Attention is limited that way. We only have so much time, energy, and attention. What we give our attention to determines our experience of life. If you give it to the primitive aspect of the mind—the egoic mind—you will suffer, not only because your thoughts are false and negative most of the time, but also because you won't be giving your time, energy, and attention to what's true, fulfilling, good, and meaningful.

There's a lot more going on in life than the thoughts in your head. Moving your attention away from the mental chatter onto what you are doing and experiencing and what is coming into your senses brings you into the present moment, where you can experience Essence. Essence is drowned out, in a sense, by the mind-chatter. Essence is *felt* and not experienced by the mind. Who you really are isn't the voice in your head.

Your attention is important. It determines your experience of reality. You have a choice about what you give your attention to once you realize you have a choice. Life is transformed by this realization. It's no mistake that you are reading this, as it is probably time for you to be more aware of your choices and their results. It's really very simple: Choosing to listen to the egoic mind takes you out of the moment and misleads and misguides you, while ignoring the mind brings you into the moment, where life is happening and wisdom and guidance are available.

When we are present to life as it is happening, our experience is full, peaceful, happy, and content. Moreover, when we are present, we discover what life wants of us and where it's taking us. When we are involved in life instead of our mind, life feels exciting and good. What an amazing difference it makes to shift our attention from the mental voice to life itself! All the love, joy, and fun you have ever experienced has been because that is what you did. You know what it's like to get lost in the moment. What you lose is the false self, and what you find is your true self—and life itself. Life is waiting for you to notice it.

9: THE NOW IS A PLACE OF NOT KNOWING

The Now is what you are experiencing right now, in the present moment. Thoughts are probably part of what you are experiencing, but thoughts and the feelings that arise from thoughts are only part of the Now. Much more is going on in *real* life. The *experience* of the moment feels more real and is more real than thought, which is simply thinking *about* experience. Thoughts about something lack the juiciness and aliveness of pure experience. They take us into a virtual reality, so to speak, and out of reality.

That wouldn't be a problem if that virtual reality didn't belong to the ego and if being involved in it didn't take us away from the experience of our true nature and its qualities: love, compassion, peace, joy, acceptance, clarity, contentment, and wisdom. The trade-off for being in the ego's virtual reality is pretty dear. We lose touch not only with the peace and contentment of our true self, but also with the flow, with where the present moment, this life, is going.

What we really are, Essence, is moving our life in a particular direction, and when we are in the Now, we naturally move in that direction. However, when we are involved in the egoic mind's virtual reality, we go where the ego takes us. That's often out of the flow because the ego drives us with its desires, and its desires and priorities are often at odds with Essence. We follow the ego's thoughts, plans, feelings, fears, and desires because we are programmed to do that, but it's time now for many to see through that programming and make a different choice.

What makes the choice of being in the moment difficult is that we have to surrender our need to know. The ego gives us a false sense of knowing, which is comforting, even though the ego doesn't really know where life is going or what will happen next. So all we really have to surrender is the *pretense* of knowing, not actual knowing.

The truth is you don't know what the next moment holds. That's both the challenge of being in the Now and, actually, the true joy of it. To be in the moment, you have to be willing to just be and respond naturally to what arises out of the flow, without pretending to know what to do next or what will happen. The thing is, you have never known what was going to happen or what to do next. Admitting that you don't know makes it possible to move out of your egoic mind and into the moment, where true happiness, peace, and alignment with Essence and its intentions are possible.

10: HAPPINESS IS A CHOICE

Much of the time, happiness doesn't seem like a choice but something that happens to us that we don't have a lot of control over. Sometimes we're happy and sometimes we aren't. Happiness is usually experienced as a feeling that is the result of getting what we want—life finally lines up with our desires, and we feel happy. The kind of happiness that is a feeling, or emotion, comes and goes like every other emotion. It's dependent on whether life is meeting our desires or not. The feeling of happiness or unhappiness is tied to desires and, therefore, to the egoic state of consciousness. We feel up or down, depending on whether life is going our way or not, according to our egoic desires.

That kind of soaring, giddy, top-of-the-world happiness feels great; the ego lives for it and wishes life would always feel that way. And it resents the fact that it doesn't. To the ego, anything less than that giddy happiness feels dull, uninteresting—and wrong. The ego's desire for life to bring constant happiness, when it doesn't, is the real cause of unhappiness. Underlying that, is anger at life—anger at not getting our way.

Depression is very much related to anger at life. When we feel that life is treating us badly and not bringing us what we want, we feel angry and sad. If these feelings go on long enough, we experience depression. Life feels not good enough, what we have seems not enough, and the possibility of getting what we want seems hopeless. Depression is a mental disorder (which may also have a biological component). Depression is what happens when we believe the ego's version of reality: "Life isn't good enough, I'm not good enough, and life and I will never be." It's an incomplete view of life. It's seeing the glass as half empty and overlooking everything that's worth celebrating.

When we are lost in the ego's point of view, it's easy to overlook the other point of view that exists simultaneously, which is a more complete and therefore truer point of view—the view of our true self, or Essence. We are free to identify with the incomplete view of reality (the ego) or with the complete view of reality (Essence). Life supports our identifying with the truth, and shows us the falseness of the incomplete view when we believe it: When we see through the eyes of Essence, we relax and feel content, peaceful, and loving; when we see through the eyes of the ego, we feel the opposite.

We are free to choose how we perceive life once we see there is a choice. This choice isn't so easy to recognize when we are giving our attention to the egoic mind and to our thoughts about *me*, or to the false self. But once we turn our attention to this very simple moment, we can begin to experience the truth—that life is good and this moment is precious.

When we choose to see life through Essence's eyes, we experience happiness, but it isn't the giddy high that the ego experiences when it gets its way. Rather, it's a subtle contentment with life as it is and a willingness to respond to life naturally, to flow along with it and enjoy where it's taking us, to welcome the adventure that it is. The ego doesn't really experience life as flowing and moving. To it, life is more like a battle to be won. But life is going somewhere, and we are part of its movement. We are co-creating with life and affecting that movement to some extent, but we aren't determining its entire course.

The beauty is that goodness underlies life, so Life's way is good and wise and can be trusted. Knowing this allows us to relax and enjoy life even when it isn't delivering what we want. When we learn to trust Life and want what Life wants for us, we experience true happiness, which only disappears if we identify with the ego again and its belief that happiness comes from getting certain desires met, from having its way.

Once we have seen that there are two possible perspectives in every moment, not just one—the ego's or Essence's—then it's possible to become free of the ego. We are given a choice, and when we realize we have a choice, freedom from the suffering caused by the ego's limited perspective is possible.

Happiness is a choice, and it's really a very simple choice: Choose the perspective that doesn't cause you to be tense, stressed, unloving, or unhappy. Choose the point of view that allows you to relax and be content and that allows love to flow. How funny it is that we are programmed to choose the opposite, when what feels right and good, what brings contentment and peace, is also the choice that leads to happiness.

11: GIVING UP THE STORY

Have you noticed how much your mind thinks about how your life is going? It's always checking to see how things line up with the way it wants your life to look. The funny thing is that life hardly ever measures up with how the story is supposed to go because it's a setup—even when life is good, something isn't good enough.

Life doesn't line up with our stories, not because life is bad or because we are doing something wrong, but because life will never line up with the ego's fantasies and desires, not completely anyway. The ego has desires that are destined to not be fulfilled. Meanwhile, life is fulfilling in all sorts of other ways.

Where would you be without this story about what you want and when you will get it? Does this story make your life go better? Does it make you happier? How can a story, which comes from the ego, which isn't wise, make your life go better or make you happier? The ego knows nothing about true happiness. Listening to it only takes us out of real life, which is unfolding beautifully according to a plan we are part of. Life is happening, and it's happening as it needs to. We operate within life as it is unfolding, we act upon it, but we don't control it, nor do we know what's best for us or those around us.

We don't have a grasp of the bigger picture—no one does. We don't get to know what life will be like, where it's going, why it is the way it is. There's so much we don't know and aren't in control of. Why pretend we are or can be in control? The ego pretends that it can make life be the way it wants it to be. But no one has succeeded at that yet. Sometimes life fulfills a desire, but more often it doesn't—and it has its own timing even when it does.

The ego tells a story about life—it's going well or not, according to its plan. However, the ego's plan is rarely aligned with the greater Plan, so what good is it? Not much good at all. So why do we pay attention to the ego's plan? Because it's in our own mind. That's pretty convincing, isn't it? Our plan is our plan. If it were someone else's plan we wouldn't believe it so easily, but we believe *our* plan. However, our plan is the ego's plan, not Essence's. How do we know? Because it's a plan. Essence's plan is not written down anywhere. It isn't known ahead of time. Any plan is the ego's. It's made-up, unreal, and therefore untrustworthy. Just because we trust our plan or believe in it doesn't make it real or trustworthy. That is the tricky thing about the ego—it's really believable even though it makes things up and isn't wise.

We can stop thinking about how our life is going and stop wondering what will happen next. These have been ineffective strategies for dealing with life. This type of thinking seems necessary, but it isn't. We believe the egoic mind offers wise guidance and a helpful perspective, when it doesn't. This illusion needs to be seen through to be free from the domination of the ego. Just seeing that the egoic mind is a false master can free us to be more present to what is real and true—to life as it is unfolding in front of us.

What is happening now? That's all we truly know about and all we need to know about. Life is coming out of the Now, and it's being moved by something unimaginably wise and good, and we are being carried forward by it. There's no need to contemplate or tell a story about where life is going or question whether it's going well. It's always moving forward according to plan—right on schedule, but not the ego's schedule.

12: THE MIND'S ENTERTAINMENT

The egoic mind loves to be entertained with the same things it tries to entertain us with: ideas, opinions, fantasies, stories, beliefs, desires, and fears. What we find entertaining within our own egoic mind is what our egoic mind is entertained by, so most media is a reflection of the egoic mind. There's nothing wrong with this; however, the truth is that we can only give our attention fully to one thing at a time, and when we are giving it to our egoic mind or someone else's, via the media, we aren't giving it to real life—what's happening and coming into our senses and, perhaps more importantly, what Essence may be communicating to us more subtly through our intuition, through knowings, and through urges and drives to take action.

Real life arises out of the flow—out of the moment—not out of the egoic mind. The egoic mind is part of life, but when we are absorbed in the egoic mind to the exclusion of others things, as so many people are, we miss out on the *experience* we are actually having. Thinking about ourselves and our life too often substitutes for real life. Using the mind in practical or creative ways isn't the problem but, rather, absorption in our thoughts about ourselves and how our life is going. Our thoughts about ourselves become our sense of who we are, and our ideas about life seem true. We end up living in a made-up reality, one where we barely pay attention to what's going on around us.

The egoic mind often finds real life—what's going on around us—boring and uninteresting. It wants to be entertained in every minute. Life is rather slow-going much of the time, whereas a movie can portray a whole life or more in two hours. In our thoughts, we also can imagine doing many different things in a matter of seconds, while real life takes time to unfold. The more time we spend absorbed in the media or in our own egoic minds, the less appealing real life is. Life doesn't have the glamour, excitement, and intensity of movies. Let's face it—most of us want to be entertained more than we want to be in the here and now. But that's natural, since we are programmed to be that way.

If it weren't for the fact that the egoic mind isn't all fun and games we might never be motivated to get away from it. The egoic mind is a great source of entertainment *and* the source of suffering too. It has a dark side. The good news is that real life is more entertaining than we *think*. Once we move out of our egoic mind and its commentary, we discover the beauty and joy inherent in life. Existence and existing are beautiful and joyful.

The egoic mind keeps us from realizing the joy and beauty of being alive. Like TV and movies, the egoic mind entertains us but doesn't fulfill us. An overdose of TV, the movies, and thinking about ourselves doesn't feel good. It leaves us feeling empty, stale, dead, and even depressed. The egoic mind isn't meant to replace real life, and we are here to discover that. We are here to discover the juiciness and joy of being alive. The dark side of the egoic mind also interferes with that, doesn't it? The egoic mind is quite the complainer. It doesn't embrace life except in those few moments when life goes its way. No, listening to the egoic mind is not always entertaining.

Listening to the mind is a habit, however, and one that can be difficult to break. Breaking it requires seeing the truth about the egoic mind—it makes us miserable as often as it entertains us. Unfortunately, it's difficult to have the entertainment without the misery. Once we allow the egoic mind to entertain us, it has us, unless we learn to detach from it at will, which usually takes a conscious choice and a practice of meditation.

We can learn to master the egoic mind, which requires realizing who we really are. We are not the egoic mind or the person our mind describes but, rather, what is conscious, awake, and living this life. We are what is aware of what's going on in the mind and of everything else. We are the awareness of everything.

When this awareness becomes strongly focused on the egoic mind and believes it, then it seems like we are the person the egoic mind tells us we are. On the other hand, when this awareness is focused on our experience rather than on our thoughts about our experience, we get a glimpse of our true nature, which is often described as Emptiness. Because this Emptiness isn't interesting to the mind, the mind turns away from the Emptiness when it is experienced. So, there are two possible experiences in any moment: the experience of absorption in your thoughts about yourself and your life or the experience of life itself. Which will you choose?

13: LOVE IS GENTLE

I was listening to a song the other day, and some of the words were "Love is gentle, and love is kind." The truth of that really touched me. We think of love as being a feeling—an emotion—but true love is more of a being and a doing, a giving, an outpouring. Love touches, love offers itself, love is gentle, and it is kind. That's how we know it. We know love by its fruits. Love gives: It listens, it caresses, it nourishes, it nurtures. It does whatever is needed of it. Love naturally responds to life as life presents itself.

Romantic love isn't like this at all. Romantic love is a giddy feeling, an excitement, an anticipation of getting something from someone. It makes us feel like a kid at Christmas—"Yippee! I'm going to get what a want!" Romance is exciting, fun, and feels wonderful, but it's not really love. It's too self-centered for that. When we are in love, we are often oblivious of the needs of others, as we have only the beloved on our mind. We become fascinated and obsessed with the beloved to the exclusion of everything else. We love the beloved, not for what he or she is, but for what we *think* that person might mean to us and to our life. We are excited because the beloved is *believed* to enhance us.

The feelings of romantic love are created by an illusion (i.e., psychological projection) and by the release of certain chemicals in the brain. Romantic feelings are a very different kind of love than true love; they are a falling in love with what we hope will be our salvation and happiness forever. That kind of love never lasts and often disappears upon getting to know someone better. If we are lucky, it turns into something truer, more real, more akin to our true nature.

It is our nature to love, to be gentle, to be kind. When all thoughts drop away or aren't given attention, love is our natural response to life. The only thing that ever interferes with love is a thought, usually a judgment or fear. These are the enemies of true love. They undermine it and eat away at it, or prevent it altogether. Love cannot exist in the ego's world of judgment and fear. And yet we, as humans, need and want love so desperately. Because of this, we learn to love for love's sake, for the joy of loving, without conditions, just because it is our nature to love. We learn to move beyond the ego's judgments and fears because doing so is the only way to get what we really want—true love. To get that, we need to return Home, and so we eventually do. We find a way to love in spite of our judgments and fears.

We discover this very simple truth: Love is an act of kindness, not a giddy feeling. Love is a natural expression of our true nature, not a feeling we get from others. The ego manipulates others to do what it wants so that it can feel love, but that's the opposite of love. Love allows others to be just as they are. It supports and nurtures, listens, and cares. Love flows toward others from within us. It exists within us and isn't something we get from others.

This kind of love is the most fulfilling thing in the world. Experiencing it doesn't require that you be beautiful or rich or healthy or intelligent or that you have a special talent or standing in life; experiencing it only requires that you express it. It's free and it frees us, and it frees others from the ensnarement of the false self. It's the greatest gift and one that doesn't cost the giver anything. It takes nothing from the giver and returns everything. This is the great secret we are meant to discover.

14: LOVE TRANSCENDS APPEARANCES

Appearances seem so important. Most of us believe that our appearance is very important, and we work very hard at looking a certain way. This is especially true for women, of course, and this conditioning is very difficult to overcome because there's a lot of fear that not looking good will have drastic consequences. For many people, appearance is a top priority and often remains that way right up until death. My mother, for instance, insisted on "putting on her face" even on her deathbed after her body had been diminished to skin and bones by cancer. Even then, she was still trying to improve herself, still not seeing the beauty that she was as this old dying woman, still not allowing herself to just be as she was.

Our appearance does affect how others initially react to us. However, it's not as important as we make it. We suffer over it and try so hard to look other than the way we do. All of this trying is exhausting and takes time and energy away from things that are more fulfilling and important in life. That's the problem—when we are consumed with our appearance, we aren't giving our attention and energy to other things that might be more meaningful, fulfilling, and rewarding. We might not discover that cultivating kindness is more rewarding than cultivating beauty. We might fail to notice the beauty that is here, within ourselves and others, just as we are.

Inner beauty and outer beauty can be at odds, since there is only so much attention and energy we have. Where your energy and attention go reflects what you value. Do you value outer beauty more than inner beauty? You might say you don't, but where are you putting your energy and attention? What are your thoughts on?

The funny thing is that others love us for our inner beauty, for the unique expression of Essence that we are, although they may be attracted to us by our outer beauty. However, that allure doesn't mean much if they don't also fall in love with us. What people fall in love with isn't our outer beauty (that's attraction or infatuation, not love), but something much more subtle—our being. They love us because they see lovable qualities that belong to Essence: goodness, creativity, kindness, joy for life, patience, compassion, courage, wisdom, strength, clarity, and so on.

The beauty of getting old with someone is the opportunity it presents to really get that appearances don't matter. You watch as your beloved changes before your eyes into an old man or old woman, but you may love him or her more than ever, not because of how he or she looks, but because you love your beloved's being—you love how he or she is in the world and with you. That's when you really get that all this emphasis on appearances is false. Appearances never were that important. You only thought they were.

Just because most people believe that appearances are important doesn't make it so. People are under the illusion that appearances are far more important than they are, which does create that reality to some extent—it makes this seem true. This illusion results in a culture that's sadly misled into putting too much energy and attention on such things. This cultural illusion makes it more difficult to discover the truth—that appearances aren't that important. But life is wise and ages us so that we can discover the truth. It is perhaps one of the greatest lessons of our lives, although it may take a lifetime to learn it.

If we realize that appearances aren't that important, then aging can be experienced as fortunate, as it gives us the gift of finally getting to relax and stop striving to improve ourselves. We finally get to put our attention on what's important—on loving others (and ourselves) just the way we are. This is the greatest gift we can give others and ourselves, and the most important thing we can do in life.

15: THINKING OF *ME*

Most thoughts are about the *me* and the story of *me*. Beliefs, desires, memories, fantasies, and opinions are all about *me* and in service to the *me*. We experience the *me* as both images of ourselves and thoughts about ourselves: what you like and don't like; what you want and don't want; what you dream; what you are angry, sad, or happy about; what you remember; what you believe; and how you see yourself, life, and others. These are also the things that most people's conversations are about. People take turns sharing thoughts about themselves with each other.

Who is the *me* at the center of all those thoughts and communications? Isn't it just an idea made up of lots of other ideas (beliefs, opinions, self-images, dreams, memories, fears, and desires)? What is it like to think those thoughts, believe them, and speak them? How does it feel when your mind is preoccupied with the *me* and when your speech is about the *me*? When you examine this, you see that absorption in the *me* is a place of suffering, a place of contraction and smallness, and much of what you say is an attempt to feel "bigger" and better about this small self.

The stories the *me* tells make us feel contracted and small because the self that these stories represent is the false self. Because these stories don't represent who we really are, we feel hollow and unfulfilled when we give voice to them. That's life's way of showing us that we aren't speaking the whole truth, that we are aligned with the false self instead of our true nature.

When you are in Essence, you are not involved with the *me*, which is just a mental construct. And although you may say *I* when you speak to someone, since language requires this, you aren't identified with the *I* that is an image, but with the *I* that exists and experiences life through you. Involvement with the *me*, which is made up of images and ideas, is the cause of suffering. Once we stop giving our attention to the *me*, we stop suffering, we stop feeling contracted and small.

You know you are aligned with your true self when you feel expansive, relaxed, at ease, at peace, content, happy, and grateful. When you feel that way, even only briefly, it's because you are absorbed in the moment, in something other than your thoughts about *me*. When you are really present to anything other than the egoic mind and its stories, you drop into Essence and feel good.

What's difficult about disregarding the thoughts about *me* and its beliefs, desires, fantasies, and memories is that we think we need these thoughts to be who we are, when we don't need them at all. In fact, they keep us from who we really are. This is quite a ruse that life (the Oneness that we are) has pulled off, but one we all eventually see through.

16: COMINGS AND GOINGS

Everything ends as quickly and suddenly as it begins. All of a sudden, you hear a bird, and just as suddenly that ends—it's over. If you notice, this isn't only true of birds singing, but of most things: Something shows up, and just as suddenly it disappears. Life is coming and going quickly, cleanly, and sometimes without our even noticing it. Life happens, and it happens by suddenly showing up and just as suddenly disappearing.

Of course, some things that show up have a longer lifespan, but even those are in constant flux during their lifespan and eventually disappear. Experiences that last awhile never remain the same while they last: If you are watching the clouds, they are constantly shifting, and then they are gone. If you are watching a ballgame, every second is different, and then it's over. If you are eating a meal, every bite is different, and then it's gone. If you are in a relationship, every moment, day, week, and year is different. Nothing stays the same. Whether it comes and goes quickly or more slowly, nothing remains the same.

The mind doesn't like it when that fun, exciting, or pleasurable moment is over. It also doesn't like the deterioration of the body as it ages, which is a more long-term phenomenon. The body is a good example of something arising and beginning a course of constant change and eventual demise. The mind clings to events, experiences, or images that have passed away, or tries to, but it can never win that game. What's over is over and can't be regained. The mind tries to retain experiences and things through memory, but memory is a poor retaining device. Like a sieve, most of the experience is lost and what remains is a poor substitute for life.

The comings and goings in life *are* life. What is life, if not these comings and goings? Life, by definition, is alive, not static, and what makes it alive is this amazing parade of events and experiences coming into our awareness and passing out of our awareness. Change is what is most constant and reliable about life.

We can always trust life to change. What we can't trust is that something will remain the same. So when the ego wants and insists that things not change, it's a ridiculous demand, like a child throwing a tantrum at the sun for coming up or going down. The ego doesn't have an accurate sense of its own power, or lack of it. Like a spoiled child, it wants its way with life. The ego doesn't believe life should be any other way than its way, so it fights with life, resisting it at every turn. And at every turn, it meets change: death and birth happening in small ways and in bigger, more dramatic ways.

Once we have seen the truth about life—that everything is constantly dying or ending and giving way to something new—it becomes increasingly difficult to argue with life. The secret to making peace with life is being willing to see the truth about it. Instead of giving your attention to what your ego wants life to be, give your attention to life itself, and you will find yourself unable to struggle against it.

The truth about life is easy to accept once we abandon the ego's perspective. Once we drop out of our thoughts *about* life and into real life, all this coming and going is just fine. In fact, it's beautiful, interesting, exciting, mysterious, and amazing. Life is good just the way it is and always has been. How silly that the mind goes on so about it! All is well and always has been. It is as it is.

17: WORKING WITH FEELINGS

It's natural that feelings show up, and it's natural to get caught up in them sometimes. When that happens, the best thing to do is just allow the feeling to be there—because it is. For the time being, it is part of what *is*, and Essence therefore embraces it and is curious about it. It's only the ego that rejects feelings and tries to get rid of or deny them or act them out. Those strategies only maintain and strengthen feelings or cause them to go underground. Rejecting, denying, or acting out feelings doesn't heal them or prevent them from recurring. Only one thing does that, and that's acceptance.

Accepting our feelings and allowing them to be here (if they are) places us outside of them, in relationship to them, rather than identified with them. The power of acceptance is that it aligns us with Essence, with the Awareness that we are, with our true self. Rejecting or denying feelings or acting them out, on the other hand, keeps us identified with the ego, which is the source of our feelings and our suffering. When we drop into Essence and into acceptance of whatever is—whether it's a feeling or a challenging situation—it's possible to bring Essence's resources to the feelings or situation. Those resources are wisdom, understanding, compassion, and curiosity, and these are what ultimately heal feelings and help them dissolve.

Essence is curious about life and everything that arises in life, including feelings. When we accept a feeling, we experience Essence's curiosity. Then it's possible to discover where that feeling came from. What thoughts created it? Feelings are caused by thoughts—by believing something—either consciously or unconsciously. If you want to heal and dissolve a feeling, then it's helpful to examine what you just thought and believed or do some deeper inquiry to perhaps uncover unconscious beliefs or assumptions you have been holding.

Our beliefs are part of our conditioning and the ego's particular spin on life. If your beliefs are creating negative feelings, then those beliefs aren't true and not serving you. Untrue or partially true beliefs have a negative outcome (negative feelings and separation from others), while truer beliefs have a positive outcome (positive feelings and love and unity with others).

Curiosity about our feelings leads to discovery and understanding, which leads to healing. Discovering the negative, untrue, and limiting thoughts behind a feeling pulls the plug on that feeling. What's it about? What mistaken beliefs or misunderstandings made you feel that way? Behind every feeling, are likely to be a number of beliefs and feelings, and uncovering each of those is the way to freedom. Once we see that the thoughts behind a feeling aren't true and not serving us, that feeling will be triggered less often and less strongly. However, we may need to see the truth about a feeling many times—each time it arises—before that emotional complex is fully healed.

Feelings stop being a problem once we realize they are avenues for discovering and releasing faulty and confused thinking. Many will be able to do this emotional work on their own, while those who have experienced abuse or other trauma will probably need to work with a professional to heal any deep emotional complexes.

18: DISIDENTIFYING WITH THOUGHTS

We are programmed to believe that our thoughts are ours, that they represent us. It's no wonder people feel bad about themselves when they believe that! So many thoughts aren't only unwise, confusing, and contradictory, but just plain mean. The ego delights in finding fault, bringing people down, and complaining. If you are identified with such thoughts, then naturally you won't feel good about yourself.

The good news is that such thoughts don't represent who we really are, but the ego and its conditioning. Everyone has an ego, and everyone's ego is selfish, self-centered, and unkind. Because people are often identified with their egos, they behave badly and so feel bad about themselves. But it doesn't have to be that way. We are actually the goodness that we also experience ourselves as. When we are loving, kind, generous, and considerate, we are expressing our true self, our true nature. This is very good news! Goodness is at everyone's core, not evil. The evil that's perpetrated in the world comes from believing our negative thoughts, from believing we are the false self, or ego.

It's possible to disidentify with the mind and identify instead with the true self, and many today are learning to do that. Two things are necessary: First, we have to see how false and useless the egoic mind is. And second, we have to have some experience of our true self. It isn't enough to have a concept of the true self because concepts belong to the mind.

The true self, or Essence, is an *experience*. Primarily, it's the experience of being aware of thoughts, feelings, and the rest of life as it is arising in the moment. That's easy! You have always been aware of thoughts, feelings, and everything else, or you wouldn't be able to speak about them. What is aware and alive in your body-mind is who you really are. You are that Awareness. You are the experience of existing and being alive and aware of your existence.

When the ego hears this, it says, "So what?" The ego isn't interested in what's real; it's only interested in its mentally created world of thought, which takes us away from the real experience of the present moment. The ego discounts the experience of our true self. It claims that experience is nothing, unimportant, and not valuable. So if you listen to the egoic mind, you will turn away from the true self and from the moment. You won't notice the experience of your true self, only the mind's version of reality.

Who we really are can only be experienced in the present moment, not through thought. When we move our attention away from thought onto anything else, we land in the present moment, the Now. The experience of being in the Now is the experience of our true self, which is felt as love, compassion, acceptance, joy, and contentment. When you experience those feelings, you know you are aligned with your true self rather than the ego. When you feel the opposite—dissatisfaction and unhappiness—you know you are identified with the ego, with your thoughts.

That understanding is powerfully freeing because, once you see that the experience of Essence and the experience of the ego are very different, you can choose which experience you will have by choosing where you put your attention. Will you give your attention to the egoic mind or to the Now? It's up to you. Making the choice to be with your *experience* rather than with your thoughts about experience will revolutionize your life.

19: WAITING

The ego isn't content with the present and is always looking to the future for some improvement. "Hope springs eternal" is true of the ego, which needs hope to cope with its negative perspective on the present. Because the way things are is rarely good enough for the ego, it fantasizes about a better future and spends the present waiting for that to come to pass. The ego's discontentment with the way things are causes it to feel bored and frustrated. It wants life to be better, and it wants it now. We have brief experiences of contentment when we get what we want, but that taste of satisfaction never lasts. Soon, the ego wants something else or more of whatever it has. No matter how life shows up, the ego isn't happy with it, or happy with it for long. This is a sad state of affairs, but life doesn't have to be that way.

What if you didn't need life to be any different than it is right now? It's possible to just say yes to life, including yes to the boredom, frustration, and longing of the ego. Those feelings may be there, but there's a lot more to any moment than the ego's discontentment. Whatever is going on is never as bad as our mind paints it. Sometimes it's incredibly challenging, but from Essence's standpoint, challenges aren't bad, but embraced for the growth they provide. Life is terribly difficult sometimes, but anything can be experienced and embraced if Essence's point of view is taken instead of the ego's.

When we are in the moment and in Essence, the sun shines or it doesn't, the work gets done or it doesn't, we have fun or we don't. Whatever the experience is, it's *experience* that Essence loves. It loves the experience of being alive and of having whatever experience we are having. The only thing that evaluates an experience is the mind, and that's where the trouble starts. Evaluating an experience takes us out of the experience and into the ego's world. In its world, life must be manipulated to get what the ego wants, and a struggle with life ensues. From Essence, there is no struggle because there's no desire for life to be any different than it is, only love for the way it is.

Loving what *is* seems preposterous to the ego. It's a good thing we aren't our ego and that we have a way out of its dissatisfaction suffering! It's a good thing that something else is here that not only accepts life as it is, but also relishes it. To Essence, all of life is delicious and precious because this same moment will never come again. You will never have this same experience again. Instead of waiting for a better moment, drop out of the mind's ideas about the present and just experience it as it is and enjoy it while you can. There's nothing to fix or change about it; it's already changing into something else. And there's no problem to solve and no place to get to.

The ego makes problems up. It defines something as a problem, and so something becomes a problem. The source of suffering is not whatever is happening, but what we tell ourselves about what's happening. Change that or don't listen to that, and you will discover that all is well and always has been. Life is trustworthy, and what you really are can be trusted to live your life beautifully. The ego tries to manage life, but it is the troublemaker and problem creator, not the problem solver.

20: HURRY UP

Because the mind is so future oriented, it's always pushing us to hurry up: "Hurry up and get there—to something better," it urges. It pushes us to move faster through whatever we are doing and on to the next task instead of being present to and enjoying whatever we are doing. When we are done, we get our reward. That's how the ego frames life.

To the ego, getting something done is the purpose of doing it. The ego is goal oriented and not interested in the journey. In service to getting things done, the mind talks to us about doing it more quickly, more efficiently, and more perfectly. The mind constantly evaluates how well and how quickly we are doing something. If we listen to its admonitions, hurry-ups, and evaluations, we won't be experiencing what we are doing, but our *thoughts about* what we are doing.

Experiencing what we are experiencing and experiencing our thoughts are very different realities, very different experiences. When we are experiencing what we are experiencing, we are at peace, relaxed, content, absorbed, with no thoughts about *me*, how *I* am doing, or any other stories, which are the ego's version of reality. Instead of experiencing reality, the ego tells a story about it, and that becomes its reality. People have a tendency to believe their own stories and take them as the truest version of reality without questioning them.

Once we become aware of the mind's tendency to tell stories, we can begin to become free of our stories, which don't served us. Many of our stories are negative, so those certainly don't serve us. Even the positive ones don't serve us because they don't represent the complete truth. They leave so much out, and something that leaves so much out is actually a lie. Moreover, such stories take us out of the moment and the experience we are having. They are intended to do that because the ego doesn't want us to be in the moment because when we are absorbed in experience, the ego—the *me*—disappears. The *me* is only a story about *me*. Without our stories, the *me* doesn't exist; only pure consciousness exists, which is what is actually living life.

The egoic mind tries to get us to hurry through life so that we don't experience life because if we actually experience it, the ego, our sense of self, disappears! So the ego hurries us on to the next moment and promises a future where we will finally be happy and able to rest. But that future never comes! It's a shell game: The mind promises us a better life if we listen to it, while it takes us out of the only thing that's real and can satisfy: the present moment. That isn't a good trade-off. The Now is vibrant, alive, rich, and ever-changing, regardless of the actual content. This vibrancy, aliveness, and richness are what fulfill us. What is unreal—thoughts, fantasies, and promises of the future—can never fulfill us; they only take us away from what can.

21: TRUE SELF-ESTEEM

The issue of self-esteem is complicated by the fact that there are two types of self-esteem: The kind that comes from the ego and the kind that comes from Essence. The ego bases its self-esteem on looking good in other people's eyes, so it tries to acquire the things—power, beauty, money, success, comforts—that make it look good and therefore enable it to feel good about itself. The trouble with this is that life may have other plans than providing us with these things, no matter how hard we try to get them. And even if we do get them, we may lose them. At death, everyone loses everything. If our self-esteem is based on how much money, beauty, success, or power we have, one day whatever gives us self-esteem is bound to be diminished. Then what happens to your self-esteem? When it's built on things that come and go, we can never just rest; we are always trying to maintain or get more of whatever we get self-esteem from. And with the ego, we can never get enough of anything. So in the end, even if we have money, power, beauty, success, or other things that make the ego feel good, it still won't feel good *enough*.

True self-esteem, on the other hand, comes from contact with Essence. When we are in contact with Essence by being present in the moment, we are naturally at peace and feel good about ourselves and about everyone and everything else. Contact with Essence is contact with the Oneness that we are. True self-esteem is esteeming everyone and everything, since everything is part of the Oneness that we are. True self-esteem leaves nothing out. It loves itself and everything else. This is the state we all want to abide in always. It's what everyone really wants. Feeling better than others because you have more beauty, power, wealth, or success than them is an empty victory. That isn't self-love; it isn't love at all. It's separation, and separation is a state of unhappiness and imprisonment, of being imprisoned by the ego and its needs and drives. And that isn't pleasant.

A lot of self-esteem isn't anything more than the ego pumping us up to compensate for not feeling good about ourselves, which is the ego's ongoing state. The issue of self-esteem is an issue that exists only because of ego identification. Without ego identification, there is no self that needs pumping up; there's only the Self, Essence, which includes everyone, and a sense of loving oneself from a place of completion and contentment.

You don't get to the experience of Essence by doing anything in particular, but more by *not* doing. What you stop doing is giving your attention to the egoic mind and its constant need for more, better, and something different. Instead, give it to this precious moment, which is complete and full of everything that will make you feel good about yourself and everyone and everything else. True self-esteem is not just loving ourselves, but loving everyone else too—because they are our Self.

22: ARE YOU CRANKY?

Crankiness is an opportunity to discover something about what you are thinking and believing. If you are cranky, ask yourself, "What am I saying to myself about myself, about life, or about others that's making me feel this way?" Beneath crankiness and anger is self-talk (either conscious or unconscious) that is complaining about the way things are and believing or wishing they were different. This is the general attitude of the ego toward life—resisting the way things are and wishing things were different. Rejection and desire are behind most anger and crankiness. The ego finds something to complain about and reject, and something to desire instead. The feelings generated by believing these complaints and desires can run anywhere from mild irritability to rage.

If we take a moment to examine the ideas behind much of our crankiness and anger, we are likely to uncover this general dissatisfaction and desire-creation mechanism of the ego. Then we can see that complaining about the way things are and wanting something different is useless when there's no chance that these complaints or desires will change the current experience. They only make the current experience more unpleasant.

On the other hand, there is another kind of dissatisfaction and desire that may be worth paying attention to. Sometimes there are things we are unhappy about that we *can* change and that, in fact, we are meant to change. When Essence is urging us in a new direction and we are resistant to seeing that new direction or making changes toward that, the result might be dissatisfaction and a desire for change that comes from our depths—dissatisfaction and desire that are meant to drive us to make certain changes that will lead to greater happiness and fulfillment. If we don't follow these deeper drives, we can end up cranky, angry, or depressed. Depression is often the result of denying the calling of our true self to do something or change something—to be true to who we really are rather than to our fears or other conditioning. Ignoring Essence's deeper drives and, instead, believing our fears and obeying our conditioning can leave us depressed and feeling empty and hopeless.

So crankiness and anger are worth examining for two reasons: If they are caused by the usual discontentment of the ego, then you can become free of these feelings by seeing that. Just notice and acknowledge that the egoic mind is doing what it was designed to do—create discontentment and desire for something different. The ability to see this, frees you from the mind's tyranny and allows you to relax and enjoy whatever is happening in the moment without resistance. On the other hand, if crankiness and anger reflect a deeper restlessness and desire for change on the part of your true self, then that needs to be honored. Essence moves us with a carrot and a stick: If we are going in Essence's direction, we feel joyful and fulfilled (carrot); if we aren't, we feel unhappy, angry, and depressed (stick).

Therefore, it is always good advice to follow your joy. And if you're not feeling joy, inquire to see if that lack of joy is the ego's usual dissatisfaction with life or if it comes from a deeper place that is prodding you to make a change or do something you might be afraid of doing. Fear always comes from the ego, and it's the most common reason for not following our Heart, our true self's calling. Dissatisfaction and crankiness could be signs that it's time to move through fears or other conditioning and courageously try something new.

23: FULFILLMENT

Everyone has a deep need for fulfillment. We seek it in various ways. Some of the things we seek fulfill us, and some don't. That is how we learn what does fulfill us, so there is no mistake in looking in so many directions for fulfillment. In pursuing things the ego wants, we discover that what the ego values is only so fulfilling. Deeper fulfillment comes from abiding by Essence's values, which are unity, love, peace, compassion, and acceptance. The beauty of these values is that they take no effort and exact no price from us, but deliver everything we really want.

The ego drives us toward getting things and being better than others. It drives us to fulfill its need for superiority, power, control, security, and comfort. In service to these goals, it pushes us to pursue wealth, fame, beauty, success, and many other things. There's nothing wrong with any of these things, of course, but they don't bring lasting fulfillment. As soon as we achieve what the ego wants, it wants even more or something else. The ego is never fulfilled because it never feels full, but empty. Trying to fulfill the ego is like trying to fill a leaky bucket: No matter how much water we put in the bucket, it's only full for a moment.

Essence isn't opposed to the things the ego wants. To be aligned with Essence doesn't mean you can't have these things or pursue them. The problem with pursuing these things to fulfill ourselves is that it doesn't work, and in the meantime, you may be missing out on doing other, more fulfilling things.

What *is* fulfilling is connecting with others, service, creativity, learning, growing, developing and using our talents, and expressing Essence through our words and deeds. We are fulfilled whenever we act in alignment with Essence and its values and intentions. Essence is moving us in certain directions. It is living us and speaking and acting through us. Allowing Essence to do that is what is most fulfilling, regardless of what that looks like. It can be something as simple as helping someone carry groceries or saying something kind. These small acts can be as fulfilling as seemingly larger acts of generosity or kindness.

The beauty is that everyone, regardless of how much money or even health or power he or she has, has the capacity to live a fulfilled life. It is how we are in our life that determines that, not what we do, have, or accomplish. Everyone has an equal opportunity for joy and fulfillment. What a blessing!

24: CHOICE

When people are very identified with their egos, they are
controlled, in a sense, by their conditioning. They respond
automatically to their thoughts, beliefs, desires, fears, and other
conditioning without evaluating them, without questioning
whether they are true or worthy guides for their behavior. Their
thoughts and feelings are their thoughts and feelings, so they act on
them. End of story. That degree of ego identification is typical of
most people. When we are identified with the egoic mind and its
conditioning to this degree, we don't feel like we have any other
choice but to follow it. Our conditioning is so unconscious or so
compelling that we just react to it.

At a certain point in our evolution, however, we begin to
become more aware of and objective about our thoughts. We begin
to wake up out of our conditioning and see the truth: Our
thoughts are not who we are and they don't have to rule our life.
Moreover, it becomes obvious that they *shouldn't* rule our life, as we
realize how negative, unwise, and untrue most of them are. This is
an amazing point in our evolution! Many people are at this point
now because the earth needs us to wake up. And many are already
awake, and their understanding and consciousness are spreading to
others.

When we begin to wake up out of the egoic mind, we realize we
have a choice to identify with the egoic mind or not. This choice is
real, and it is crucial in the process of waking up. Once you begin
to awaken, you can agree to participate in the awakening process
with your will more fully or less fully. You can facilitate the process
of waking up or slow it down by how you use your will, by what

you choose. The *you* that can choose to be present in the moment rather than be ego identified is the real you, although this *you* still sometimes gets lost in ego identification. Waking up out of ego identification is similar to waking up in the morning and being drowsy: You are a little awake, but you still slip back into sleep and then awaken again and then slip back into sleep. Until we become more stabilized in the awakened state, we move back and forth between ego identification and awakeness.

While you are waking up, it's important to recognize that you have a choice, at least sometimes, to stay awake. In any moment, you can choose to be involved with your thoughts, or you can be in the moment and *experience* the moment free of the mind's commentary. Being awake is simply being present to the experience you are having instead of to your thoughts *about* that experience.

Once you are awake and living mostly in the Now, your actions and speech happen spontaneously without a lot of thought or evaluation. When you are living in the Now, choosing and doing just seem to happen. There is no longer a sense of trying to make a choice, which is the experience the ego has. The ego is always struggling with various options, weighing them, evaluating them, and creating a lot of confusion around choice-making. When we are in Essence, the experience is very different from that. We easily flow with life, acting and speaking naturally and wisely, without the confusion and debate created by the mind. There's no sense of *me* doing something, but just doing. That's what spiritual teachers mean when they say there is no doer, because when we are in Essence, that is the experience.

To sum up: There are two stages in our evolution when we experience a sense of not having a choice: When we are so ego identified that our conditioning runs us without our questioning it, and when we are so aligned with Essence that choosing happens without our conscious concern. At both stages, choosing just happens, but one is the ego choosing and one is Essence choosing. However, when we are waking up out of ego identification and just learning to be in Essence, the experience is one of seeing that we have a choice of falling back into identification with the egoic mind or being in the moment with Essence.

25: MISSING OUT

The reason we find thoughts about ourselves and others so compelling, besides the fact that we are programmed to pay attention to them, is that we believe we need them to function—and we enjoy thinking. Nevertheless, such thoughts come from the ego, and we don't need those thoughts, and we are better off without them.

We think that if we don't pay attention to the voice in our head, we will miss out on something, but what we miss out on when we give our attention to that voice is real life, the life beyond the ego's mental world. The ego doesn't have a very high opinion of real life, and neither do we when we are identified with the ego. Life without thoughts seems boring, uninteresting. But that's only because we don't stay in real life long enough to really experience what it has to offer. We often have one foot in and one foot out of our present moment experience: one foot in the mind and one foot in what is real.

We tend to believe that thinking supplies everything we need: wisdom, insight, information, guidance, planning, and fun. What more could you ask for? If paying attention to the egoic mind could really provide these things, then this voice in our head would be indispensible and a true friend. However, it fails miserably at this. Even the fun often comes at quite an expense. The egoic mind pretends to be able to provide these things, and we are programmed to believe it can, but it doesn't deliver what it promises. Even once we see this, we may still give this voice in our head our attention, just in case it comes up with something good—maybe the next thought is the one that will change everything!

Everything we really want to know—what will happen, why things have happened, and what to do next—isn't known by the mind. Let this sink in a moment, because we are deeply conditioned to believe that the egoic mind has those answers. What if you really knew that it doesn't have any of the answers you are looking for? Instead, it is what raises those questions and wants so badly to know the answers—but it doesn't have them.

If you take a look, you discover that most of your thoughts are an attempt to figure out what's going to happen, what to do in the future, or how to deal with the past, either by trying to understand the past, take a position on it (tell a story about it), or change it, which is impossible. All these thoughts are fruitless. We can't know the future, we can't figure out what to do in that unknown future, and we can't do anything about the past because it no longer exists. Just stop a moment again, please, and really take this in. These thoughts only waste our time and energy and take us out of real life. When you really see that, you can begin to be done with them. But there's one more thing you need to do.

Once you have seen how pointless your thoughts about the past and future are, you need to fall in love with the present. If you don't, you will go back to your thoughts about the past and future out of habit and because there's some enjoyment in them. Before we are able to leave those thoughts behind, we have to have a very good reason to do something else. The egoic mind won't give you a reason to pay attention to the present because the ego (the mind-created self) disappears when you are in the moment, and it doesn't want to disappear. You—the real you, the *you* that is awakening—have to find a reason to pay attention to the present.

The reason to pay attention to the present is that the present is the only thing real. The past and future are just thoughts, and thoughts about them are just more thoughts. The past and future aren't real because they don't actually exist when our mind is still and we are just present to what's arising now, in the moment. When we do that, we discover how pleasurable it is to be present. But it can take a lot of practice to stay present long enough to experience the pleasure of being present. Is that pleasure worth giving up your thoughts about the past and future, your worries and fears, your plans and your fantasies?

When you really see the truth about your thoughts and the truth about being present, the choice is clear. But it can take a while before we are convinced that thoughts aren't what they seem to be and that the present isn't the boring experience our mind assumes it is. Awakening is the process of waking up out of the imaginary world created by our thoughts and living in the here and now, free of the domination of those thoughts. What an amazing transformation of consciousness that is, and what a blessing it is that you are experiencing awakening in this lifetime.

26: FREEDOM

Even those who have little freedom physically, perhaps because of incarceration or health limitations, have a kind of freedom that can never be taken away. In fact, that freedom is often discovered in instances of extreme physical limitation. When we are prohibited from living our life as we would like to, we discover what is forever and always free: consciousness.

Our consciousness has never been bound by a body or by anything. Our consciousness—or Consciousness, which is what we really are—is only temporarily identified with our particular body-mind. That body-mind and the life it is leading isn't particularly important to Consciousness. After all, Consciousness, or the Oneness, has manifested in every possible form and non-form for its own exploration and pleasure. How our particular form looks, what state it's in, and how our life is going is not an issue for Consciousness. It created it all and loves it all, just as it is. It intends to have exactly the experience we are having within our body-mind.

This joy isn't simply theoretical. The joy Consciousness experiences can be experienced by us, no matter what our circumstances are. If we aren't experiencing it, it's only because we aren't paying attention to it, but to the complaints and discontentment of the egoic mind, which tries to define our life and our experience for us. Consciousness defines all experience as good and worthwhile. That is its truth, and it can be our truth, not just in theory, but in experience.

We have the freedom to choose what we give our attention to and what we believe about ourselves, our situation, others, and life.

This is a tremendous responsibility, as it determines to a great extent what our experience of life will be. No matter what our circumstances are, we have the freedom to accept them, to not argue with reality, but allow ourselves to have the experience we are having—because we are!

Arguing with life is what the ego does, and that creates inner stress and unhappiness, which is so unnecessary. You don't have to like your circumstances to accept them, and accepting them doesn't mean they will remain the same. You only have to be willing to have the experience you are having, just as Consciousness is. When we align ourselves with the view of life that Consciousness has, we feel its joy and love for life, and that's all we ever need to be happy.

Freedom is truly a state of mind or, rather, a state of no mind, or ignoring the mind's complaints about life. We are already free and always have been. We have been given this great gift of choice: the freedom to choose how we see life and respond to it. As a result, everyone eventually learns to see life through the eyes of the true self and dismiss the false self's version, which is the source of all suffering. Happiness is under your control more than you may realize. You have more power than you may think—you have the power to *not* think, to ignore your thoughts, and to experience the gift that this life is.

27: WHAT ARE YOU RESPONSIBLE FOR?

What are you responsible for? This is an important question because the ego, the conditioned self, tends to take responsibility for more than what it's actually responsible for, and that leads to suffering. For instance, many feel responsible for other people's feelings. But how can you be responsible for other people's feelings and reactions? Others are free to respond however they will to you. You aren't in control of their feelings and reactions, so how can you be responsible for them?

It's not that you shouldn't care about how you affect others, but there are times when our actions aren't going to be received well by others even though they are right and true for us. When we are following our Heart, others might not be happy with that, and they might try to talk us out of it by reacting badly toward us.

Do you not follow your Heart because someone isn't happy about that? Are you responsible for the sadness or anger someone feels about your choice? Just because someone doesn't like what you are choosing, does it mean your choice is bad for that person or for you? If a choice is right for our soul's growth, then it's probably right for the souls of those involved with us. The negative reactions of their egos aren't reason enough to not follow your Heart.

There will always be people who like and don't like what we do. If we were to try to accommodate everyone's preferences whenever we did something, we would be frozen in place, which is why some people feel stuck. Our choices can't be based on pleasing others, although their well-being is likely to be part of any decision. Other people often suppose they know what's best for us, but most people operate from their egos and therefore don't.

Life has a beautiful way of teaching us through the choices we make. We receive feedback from life about our choices, which causes us to be happy with a choice or change it. Everyone moves through life this way—blind, in a sense, since no one really knows where their choices will lead. No one has a crystal ball. We learn from the past, but the past doesn't predict the future.

We are responsible for our choices and for learning from them. The rest isn't in our control. We aren't in control of what will happen or how others will respond to our choices. We aren't in control of anything but our choices, including what we choose to conclude about ourselves, others, and life. We are the master of our inner universe, and we do determine how we view our experiences and what we will do about them. Our inner universe is our responsibility. The outer universe is not.

The good news is that something else, an unimaginable Intelligence, is in control of the universe, if not individuals' specific responses. The course of the universe is being shaped by something so immense that we can't begin to comprehend it, and it is something we can trust. We can trust that Intelligence to guide us, and we can trust it to guide others toward greater love and peace, because that is where life is headed. One way or another, life is moving in that direction. That is something we can be certain of, but not something we are responsible for.

That Intelligence takes into account the good of the Whole, all of its manifestations, as it moves life forward through all of us. It works through us and with us to bring about its intentions for life, and its intensions are all good. One of its intentions is that we learn and evolve as a result of our choices, and so we do, and so do others. As they choose how to react to us, they learn they are creating their experience of reality by how they respond. Eventually everyone learns they are responsible for their feelings and reactions, and no one else.

28: TRUTH

How do you tell if a belief is true? Most beliefs aren't true, simply because no belief can reflect the complete truth. For instance, the belief that men are physically stronger than women is a generalization that is often true, but not always, which is the case with most beliefs: They are often true, but not always.

The problem with beliefs that aren't always true is they can distance us from what *is* true in the moment. What's true is what is true in the present moment, not what was true in the past or what might be true in the future. When we hold a belief, we often trust it more than we trust what's true in the moment, and that's the problem. And when we are focused on a belief, we may not notice what's true in the moment.

The truth is whatever brings us closer to love and unity. Many beliefs separate us from others because they represent a stance for or against something. That is, of course, the ego's stance; it tends to take a stand for or against something. The Heart, or Essence, on the other hand, doesn't move through life based on beliefs, but lets love guide the way. What opens your Heart? Does a belief cause you to love more, not only yourself and others, but also life itself? That is the true test of a belief. Any belief that does that is a keeper. Any belief that does the opposite isn't worth our attention.

Our beliefs are important. They determine our *experience* of reality to a large extent. They can also determine reality, as many beliefs become self-fulfilling prophecies. Our beliefs are therefore powerful—if we believe them. If you can be aware of your conditioned beliefs and hold them lightly, they don't have to be a problem.

We can't really do away with our beliefs. Like all thoughts, beliefs arise out of nowhere, and we can't prevent that. What we can do is notice our beliefs, evaluate them, and then dismiss them or apply them. A good guideline is to accept a belief only if it brings you closer to love and unity and doesn't take you away from that. You will discover that few beliefs pass this test. Most beliefs, because they come from the ego, are negative and separating. They take us away from love and away from peace, within ourselves and in relationship to others.

We actually don't need any beliefs at all. To be loving and in Essence, we don't have to believe anything; we only have to not believe what the ego believes. When we are in Essence, it acts and speaks through us and doesn't need beliefs to shape its speech and action. It naturally acts and speaks from love. To be loving, we don't have to reshape our beliefs to make them more loving, although that can help. We only have to move out of the mind and its beliefs and live from Essence, which knows perfectly how to love and live life. Beliefs haven't helped us live better; they've only interfered with living truly and purely in the present moment, which has all the wisdom we need.

29: OUR HOMING DEVICE

We have a built-in guidance system. That system doesn't work through the mind, but through the body, through a sense of expansion or contraction of our energy. Our energy registers whether something is true or not by either expanding and relaxing or contracting and tensing, which is often felt physically as well. When we are identified with the mind and its negativity, our energy contracts, and our physical body also contracts and becomes tense. On the other hand, when we are in Essence, our energy feels expansive and relaxed, and so does our body.

Essence guides us and brings us Home through contraction and expansion. Contraction and tension don't feel good, and expansion and relaxation do. Life uses this guidance system to point us away from what's false and toward what's true. Through positive feelings of expansion, relaxation, and peace, we are pointed Homeward.

The ego, which operates through the mind, is the false self, and it's called that for a reason. What it has to offer is mostly false and doesn't bring true happiness or peace, but takes us away from happiness and peace. Essence, on the other hand, while not as obvious as the false self because it doesn't communicate through thoughts, is nevertheless very present in our life, and it offers us true happiness and peace. Essence is, in fact, what lives our life, and the false self is an imaginary self that obscures our true nature.

We are meant to see that what the false self values—superiority, power, and control—aren't worthwhile values. We are shown this through the experience of contraction and tension when we align ourselves with those values or with thoughts that represent them.

When we align ourselves with love, compassion, acceptance, and peace, we feel expansive, relaxed, and at ease. Through relaxation, joy, peace and a sense of ease and expansion, Essence communicates what's true, real, and meaningful about life.

What a blessing it is that life communicates this way! It means that everything you really want and everything that will make you happy and bring you peace feels good and right, while everything that brings unhappiness, separation, and pain feels bad. The strange thing is we have been programmed to distrust this guidance system and listen, instead, to the egoic mind. So people tend to go after the very things that will never satisfy them or bring true happiness, even though the pain in doing so is obvious. Many don't realize that there's something more trustworthy than the mind, and that is Essence.

In every moment, Essence is communicating our state of consciousness to us: When we are in Essence, we experience peace and contentment; and when we are identified with the ego, we experience confusion and discontentment. Contentment or discontentment show us what we are identified with—Essence or the ego. That contentment and discontentment are also felt energetically as expansion and relaxation or contraction and tension. If you pay attention to your state moment-to-moment, you can become aware of whether you are identified with Essence or the ego.

Once you realize you are identified with the egoic mind, you can choose differently. Once you realize you are contracted because you believed something the mind has told you, you can examine what you were thinking and discover its falseness, which frees you from identifying with those thoughts. Inquiry such as this frees us from ego identification.

Feelings of discontentment and tension are a sign that we need to inquire into certain thoughts we have believed and identified with. Those thoughts aren't true or they wouldn't have led to contraction and tension. Once you understand that contraction indicates an untrue thought, then dismissing thoughts that cause you to contract becomes much easier. Such thoughts lose their power to grab you. If you ignore thoughts that cause you to contract often enough, they will appear less frequently, and you will eventually be free of them.

30: BEFRIENDING FEELINGS

Some of our conditioning is useful and serves a purpose, such as, "Look both ways before you cross the street" and "Don't put anything but a plug into an electrical outlet." Some conditioning is useful or at least neutral, but conditioning that makes us feel bad, fearful, sad, angry, guilty, hateful, regretful, jealous, vengeful, shameful is not. We don't need the thoughts that create those feelings, and we don't need those feelings. Life on this planet would be vastly improved without them.

Because we can't do away with a negative feeling once it's there, the only choices for dealing with it are to reject it, act it out, or accept it. Accepting a feeling means allowing it to be there for as long as it's there. Doing that weakens it and lessens its capacity to dominate us, either consciously or unconsciously. Rejecting a feeling, on the other hand, causes it to persist, if not consciously, then unconsciously. And acting a feeling out only reinforces it. While acceptance allows the pool of negative feelings that we all carry to be drained, rejecting or acting out a feeling maintains that pool and causes it to spill over.

Accepting our feelings and allowing them to be there without feeding them or telling stories about them helps them heal and evolve. Eventually, we stop creating feelings with our thoughts because we see our feelings for what they are: programmed reactions to beliefs we hold, which are also programmed and automatic, like all conditioning.

Our evolution requires that we become conscious of our thoughts and the feelings generated by those thoughts. Once we have become aware of and more objective about our thoughts and feelings, we can become free from the ego, and the ego stops functioning or functions only minimally. Until then, we will continue to experience negative feelings from time to time. When negative feelings do come up, the thing to do is befriend them.

"Befriending" is a good word because no matter how badly a friend might behave, we treat a friend with care and curiosity, and we want to support his or her growth. If we take the same attitude toward an emotion, it will cease to be a problem for us. By bringing compassion and curiosity to a feeling and an intent to heal it, our relationship to that feeling is changed, and as a result, the feeling changes. Furthermore, such a relationship provides an opportunity to discover more about the feeling—what caused it and what keeps it in place—by dialoguing with it, just as we might dialogue with a friend.

Such dialogues and inquiries aren't done with the mind, but with the Heart. When we are a good friend, we listen to our friend. Being a good friend to a feeling means listening to it, being present to it, and seeing what it might have to reveal. By listening, we give it space to speak to us. What speaks is actually our own wisdom, or Essence, which reveals to us intuitively what we need to know about that feeling.

When we work with feelings this way, the results can be very rich. Feelings become friends instead of problems. They are friends that help us heal and evolve our conditioning. It's up to us to befriend our feelings, however, because like an angry and irrational friend, feelings aren't very likeable at first. But it's at those times, as with friends, that our feelings are most in need of our compassion, curiosity, and acceptance.

31: BOREDOM

Boredom is a common experience produced by the ego. It is an egoic state of dissatisfaction plus a desire for something either unspecified or denied. If the desire were clear and able to be pursued, then action would take the place of inaction. Instead, boredom is a state of inaction plus restlessness. With boredom, it isn't clear what we want to do, so we remain stalled, but discontent with doing nothing. If we dropped out of that state of consciousness, we would either enjoy doing nothing or find the clarity and motivation to do something. Boredom is a muddled state, where we feel discontent but unclear about what would change that.

Fortunately, boredom never lasts for long because life has a way of moving forward. Things arise within us or outside of us to do, so our attention shifts away from feeling bored, and we stop feeling that way. After all, boredom is just a feeling, with no basis in reality, and it passes, like every other thought and feeling. Realizing that boredom comes and goes, like the weather, makes it less likely that we will make it into a problem and suffer over it. It's not the problem we *think* it is.

The ego makes boredom into a problem: It creates it, and then it agonizes over it. How interesting and ironic that is! But then, every uncomfortable feeling—fear, anger, resentment, sadness, guilt, shame, jealousy, envy, hatred—is created by the ego and then agonized over. Uncomfortable feelings become a problem to solve, and trying to solve such problems takes a lot of energy.

Boredom is less uncomfortable than many other negative emotions, but it can still feel problematic if we take it personally. The problem with boredom or any other feeling actually comes from taking such feelings personally. Feelings become a problem when they are *our* feelings because we think they mean something about us or our life: Having feelings means you have a problem, and if you have a problem, there must be something wrong with you. Now, that really *is* a problem! Having feelings makes us feel inadequate about ourselves, which is one reason we want to get rid of them.

What if you let boredom or any other unpleasant feeling just be there, as if it belonged to someone else or to no one? That feeling is just one more thing going on in the moment, and it isn't any more personal than the temperature of the room, the time of day, or the weather, which are also constantly changing. Our feelings are like the weather: unpredictable, always shifting, and impersonal.

Our feelings aren't personal. They are created by our thoughts, which come into our mind, unbidden. We aren't the cause of our thoughts or feelings—our conditioning is—although we are responsible for our reactions to them. You can become free of automatically and unconsciously responding to your thoughts and feelings by simply seeing the truth about them. By not believing and identifying with them, they lose their power to be a problem for you. However, if you aren't able to disidentify with your thoughts and feelings by not believing them, then some emotional healing may be necessary first.

32: WHAT YOU REALLY KNOW

What we really know is mostly what comes in through our senses, and that has a limited radius. How far do your senses extend? We may see mountains many miles away, but we don't really know what the experience of being on that mountain is until we are there, within yards of it. The same is true of everything else we experience. We only really know what our senses tell us about our immediate surroundings. We may know that the ground is damp, the tree is starting to bud, the sun is shining, and the air is cool, but there isn't a lot more we can say with surety about life except what our senses tell us about our immediate surroundings.

Outside of our immediate sensory experience is our acquired knowledge, suppositions, and assumptions, all of which are stored in the brain and may or may not be true in this particular moment. Most of the things we think we know, such as what we are going to do tomorrow, next week, or next year, or even what happened in the past, are imaginations, plans, ideas, and memories and not something we actually know. Even our knowledge is more limited than we assume: We assume the earth is round because it has been, but we can't assume it will be round tomorrow. The earth may not even exist tomorrow. We don't even really know that.

We create a sense of ourselves, our life, and our world with our ideas about ourselves, our life, and our world, but these are just ideas—imaginations—when all we really know about life is what's coming in through our senses. These ideas are useful, of course, and they are obviously meant to be part of our experience as human beings. Without the ability to think and imagine, we couldn't be the creators that we are. And yet, all this imagining and thinking takes us away from real life and from the real experience of ourselves as life itself. It takes us away from the here and now, from reality. We live, instead, in a mental world, where we think we know things and we pretend we know what will happen.

The distancing from our true self and from reality that thinking causes makes us feel fearful in the world. When we are detached from our core, from Essence, we are detached from our innate trust of life and our natural responsiveness to life. Too much involvement in knowledge and thought leaves us responding to life from our knowledge, beliefs, and opinions rather than from our innate wisdom. The simplicity of living close to our true nature is enlivening, refreshing, peaceful, and kind, and our world needs this so very much these days. We need this.

So notice how your real world, your real experience, actually extends only a few yards in every direction, and that will help you live more in the here and now. Beyond those few yards where your senses reach, you don't know, you only assume you know. Notice how much you really don't know—it's a lot! Instead of being a problem, this is actually a wonderful discovery. You can relax and be at peace—you don't know and you don't need to know anything more than you do. You can leave this life up to the life that is living you and see what it will do next, when you aren't letting yourself be run by your mind, your beliefs, your judgments, and your knowledge. Get to know the being that you are by realizing that it is alive right here and now and sensing life and that everything else is what you pretend life to be.

The being that you are is wise and knows how to live life, but it doesn't let you know ahead of time what it's up to or where it's taking you. This inner knowing doesn't come through your ordinary senses. But when the mind is quiet, it is felt strongly and clearly, and it feels very real. The knowing that comes from the being that you are is a moment-to-moment knowing, not a pretend knowing. It shows up in the moment and guides you for that moment, until another knowing shows up. You could say it's an ephemeral knowing, a knowing that lasts as long as it needs to, and then disappears when no longer needed. This knowing is trustworthy because it's real, because it comes out of the here and now. Pretend knowings make the ego feel safe because the ego needs and wants to feel safe. But we don't need our pretend knowings in order to be safe, since life is trustworthy and safely evolving us toward greater wisdom and love no matter what is happening.

33: TRUE HAPPINESS IS FREE

So much of what makes for true happiness is free, available to rich and poor alike. What gives Essence joy, and therefore gives us joy, is experiencing life, expressing ourselves, creating, growing, learning, and serving others. For instance, it costs nothing to experience the beauty of nature, to sing, or to speak kindly to others or in other ways serve them. Many of the things we can do for others don't cost anything except maybe time and energy. There is great joy in experiencing, expressing, creating, growing, learning, and serving. Furthermore, we can do these things again and again, we can't do them too much, and we won't run out of opportunities to do them.

The beauty of this planet and the miracle of its life forms can be a never-ending source of joy if we take time to notice what's around us, not only with our eyes, but also with our other senses, which were given to us for just that purpose. Even unpleasant sensory experiences are amazing and appreciated by Essence. What a range of experiences is possible here on this planet! Essence created everything, and it revels in experiencing what it has created. When we are in Essence, we feel that joy and amazement.

The mind overlooks so much: "I've seen that. I know that," it concludes. It labels things, presumes to know them, then shifts attention onto something else, most likely a thought about the past or future or a desire. The ego isn't interested in experiencing life; it's only interested in its version of life and in getting what it wants. If the ego doesn't see something or some experience as potentially enhancing to it or useful in achieving its goals, the ego quickly loses interest in it.

But Essence's goal *is* experience. Its approach to life is very different from the ego's. When you are no longer identified with the egoic mind to the extent that most people are, your experience of life will be very different. You will see life from Essence's eyes instead of the ego's, and what Essence sees is beauty everywhere because it loves life and feels such gratitude to have a body that is capable of sensing it.

Without a body-mind, the Creator can't experience its creations, at least not the same way. The Creator had to become alive within its own creations to really experience creation, and that's what it has done. It has taken on a unique body-mind to have a unique experience through each of us. What a miracle that is, and what an amazing Intelligence we belong to. Life is a great gift, and that gift is relished by Essence. The Creator is alive in us as Essence.

The Creator doesn't know exactly what will unfold in creation, which makes life especially interesting. It doesn't know how life will unfold because it has given its sentient creations, like us, free will. We are free to choose to align with Essence or identify with the ego, which is an illusion that has been created to make things interesting.

It's our purpose to experience this life, and life can be joyful when we allow the experience we are having instead of reject or fight it. The ego is designed to reject life, but we are meant to learn to say yes to it all, as Essence does. That is the secret to life. Secrets are hidden, and this one is hidden by the ego. This world is a bit of a puzzle to solve, and we are given all the clues we need to solve it. The biggest clue is to follow your joy because when you do that, you will be following Essence instead of the ego.

34: AN OPPORTUNITY TO LOVE

Every moment is an opportunity to love. Of course, the ego doesn't see it that way. It sees every moment as an opportunity to try to get what it wants. The ego sees the moment through the lens of its desires: "Am I getting what I want now?" it asks. The answer is usually no. Even when the ego is getting what it wants, it worries that that will end, or it imagines how that could be even better. To the ego, the moment isn't an opportunity to love, but an opportunity (hopefully) to get. The ego has it backwards, which is why it is never happy. It doesn't do what will make it truly happy, only what it imagines will make it happy. It believes that happiness lies in getting, not giving, and that is the great misunderstanding.

Essence knows only love. It doesn't know how to do anything but love. It had to create a false self that did the opposite to have the experience of not loving. Essence can't help but love, so it wants the experience it is having through us, whatever that is. It says yes to it because saying yes to life is what we do when we love life.

When we say yes to the experience we are having, we become fully involved in it without the mind's rejection of it or complaints about it, and that involvement results in loving it. Whenever we are fully involved in something without the ego's resistance to it—without thoughts coloring the experience or taking us out of it—we fall in love with life. Have you ever gotten so engrossed in a movie or novel, even a sad one, that you lost all sense of yourself and, at the same time, entirely enjoyed the experience? Essence's experience of life is like that. It loves getting lost in the character and story. It enjoys the changeableness of life, the unpredictability, the drama, the play, and the possibilities that exist in every moment. What will happen next? As in the best movies and novels, we don't know. That's what makes life fun.

Love, in this sense, is not an emotion but comes from jumping into experience fully and being willing to really have the experience you are having. Every moment is an opportunity to jump in with both feet, without holding back by evaluating or questioning the experience. The egoic mind inserts itself into every moment, or tries to, by evaluating it, worrying about it, or telling a story about it. That commentary doesn't enhance life or keep us safe; it simply distracts us from the experience and prevents us from being fully involved in it. Most people have one foot in their minds, so to speak, and one foot in their experience, which doesn't feel the same at all as having both feet in an experience.

You know what it feels like to have both feet in an experience. That's when you feel most happy, most free, and when life feels the juiciest. For most people, those moments are brief, although memorable. Life can be and is meant to be intensely alive like that all the time. It's a matter of recognizing that every moment is an opportunity to say yes to life.

When you do say yes to life, you enjoy it, regardless of what's going on. You enjoy the moment for its uniqueness and unpredictability and for how it evolves you—because life changes us when we let ourselves experience it, and it's meant to change us. Life takes us along with it. It is taking each of us on a ride. We can go kicking and screaming, which is what the ego does, or we can say yes to life and enjoy the ride. The good news is that we can relax because Life knows what it is doing. We are in good hands.

35: FAITH

There are two kinds of faith, one is rather blind, and the other is clear seeing. When people believe something because they are told to without having an inner knowing of it, that's blind faith. On the other hand, when people believe something because they have an inner knowing that can't be shaken, that is clear seeing. It's natural to have faith in what seems clear and true to us, and that's what can be trusted. What can't be trusted are other people's ideas and beliefs, or even our own. Beliefs are ideas, and most are conditioning, which may or may not be true.

Beliefs have to be tested within. They have to pass an inner truth test. Problems arise when people swallow beliefs without testing them. They apply them blindly to situations, like a formula. But life is not that simple. It requires ongoing testing in the moment. What is true now? And is it still true now?

The biggest problem with beliefs is that they are true sometimes but not always. So if we assume that a belief is always true, it won't serve us, and it may even create trouble for us. An example is the belief that we shouldn't lie. Most people would agree that telling the truth is a sound ethical principle. And yet, if we always told the truth, that would surely hurt others unnecessarily at times. Which ethical principle supersedes the other? Do you lie and hurt someone, or do you, out of love, withhold the truth? This is a common moral dilemma. If you check inside when such a dilemma arises, you will find the answer. Chances are you will discover that being loving is more important than being completely honest. When you look inside, love usually wins out over moral beliefs or tenets, even though such tenets are intended to promote kindness and good behavior.

How can so much bad behavior—killing and other injustices— come from religious and other beliefs? It happens when people adhere blindly to beliefs without checking out the truth, which resides in them, in that moment. If those fighting a war were to check inside for the truth, most would throw down their arms. But they have faith in what they are doing. Is that blind faith or clear seeing? That can only be answered by that individual in that moment.

The good news is that you always know the truth. We all have an inner guidance system that gives us accurate feedback about what to do in any situation. We don't need moral codes to act rightly. In fact, as history has shown, blind adherence to religious beliefs has fueled many wars and other atrocities. We don't need rules and codes to control our behavior. We only need to check within to discover what is right—and then follow that. "Following that" is the hard part.

The ego doesn't want to follow what is right, good, and loving. Instead, it distorts moral codes and beliefs to serve its ends, and the result is wars and other hurtful acts. The problem isn't in the moral codes, but in what the ego does with them. How can moral codes that encourage people not to kill or harm each other be a problem? They are a problem only when the ego misapplies them, distorts them, and uses them to justify the very thing those codes advise against. A prime example of this is pro-life activists who murder doctors who perform abortions.

No matter how much evil is perpetrated in the name of faith or religious beliefs, we always know the truth, if we are willing to acknowledge it. Our inner guidance system never sleeps, but is always communicating its wisdom to us. That is why goodness and the truth ultimately prevail. That guidance system can be ignored, but it can't be disabled. Besides, not following it only leads to suffering, which eventually points everyone back to the truth.

36: PREFERENCES

Everyone has preferences. Even after spiritual awakening, people have preferences. They are part of our programming and part of what makes us unique. That programming gives the Oneness a unique experience through each of us. The ego causes us to suffer over our preferences, however, by making them more important than they are. The ego leads us to believe we won't be happy if our preferences aren't met, and that simply isn't true, unless we choose to be unhappy. Interestingly, believing we can't be happy unless we get our preference met can be a self-fulfilling prophecy: We become unhappy because we expect to be unhappy or because we believe we should be unhappy. The ego turns simple preferences into something to suffer over.

Most preferences are a matter of taste, which varies from person to person. So how important can they be to our happiness? If we prefer chocolate ice cream and are given vanilla instead, how bad is that? Many people would rather have vanilla, so it can't be that bad. What makes it bad is comparing chocolate to vanilla or holding an idea of chocolate while eating vanilla. The problem isn't in the experience of vanilla, but in what the mind does with that experience. The mind interferes with experiencing vanilla ice cream with images and ideas of something else. If uncluttered by those images, eating vanilla ice cream instead of chocolate is just a different experience, not an inferior one, or at least not a reason to suffer.

That's a simple example of a taste preference, but the same applies to more weighty preferences. For instance, you might prefer that people aren't late or that they answer your emails promptly or that they pick up after themselves. Those are also conditioned preferences. Every preference is a desire: We desire one thing over another. Desires tend to become emotionally charged, while preferences are less likely to. Preferences could be considered mini-desires, but preferences, like desires, can cause suffering if we take them too seriously.

So what happens when someone is late and you prefer that he or she be on time? Notice how the egoic mind creates suffering over this: "How can he be so inconsiderate? Doesn't he know I have other things to do today? He's so selfish. He never follows through on his promises. I can't count on him. I'm never going to make a date with him again. Why does this always happen to me?" When we buy into such thoughts, the ego keeps piling them on. It goes on and on in an attempt to stir up emotions. If one statement doesn't work, the ego tries another.

The ego wants to stir up emotions because emotions justify its statements. Feelings make the ego's story seem true and justified, and there's nothing the ego likes better than feeling right and self-righteous. All of the stories the ego tells when it doesn't get what it wants are in service to feeling right and self-righteous or generating some other emotion, which keeps us involved with it. Such stories aren't the truth.

Once you realize this, you don't have to indulge in those stories. You don't have to go down that road. You've gone that way many times before, and what has it gotten you? Instead, just acknowledge you have a preference for something else. After that, just have the experience you are having, without a lot of thoughts about it. Eat that vanilla ice cream and see what it's like or wait for that person and really notice everything that's part of that experience rather than thinking about it or about something else. Just be there in the experience you are having. It's always good!

37: LIFE BRINGS YOU WHAT YOU NEED

What if you believed and knew at your very core that life brings you what you need? That isn't what the ego believes. The ego doesn't trust life and feels solely responsible for our survival—as if there is nothing else here supporting us—and it convinces us of this. The egoic mind plans, strategizes, and worries about survival. It scares us into believing we can't survive if we don't listen to it.

It's not that the ego's plans and strategies don't work—they often do—but often at the cost of our happiness, peace, and joy. We don't need the ego's plans because something else is living our life and everyone else's just beautifully. The Intelligence behind life brings us everything we need to support ourselves and learn what we are here to learn.

At times, the Intelligence behind life brings us challenges, but when it does, it also provides ideas, wisdom, inner strength, people, and other resources to help us cope with and learn from those challenges. Help is also available from beings in other dimensions who guide us, whose purpose is to help shape our life. So although life in this dimension is difficult and even dangerous at times, we are given what we need to see our way through the challenges and come out stronger, wiser, and more compassionate.

The ego doesn't acknowledge the help that life provides. It overlooks or minimizes the strength, wisdom, and support that are available. The ego fights against life and argues with its challenges. It complains and feels victimized and angry. This resistance to life makes seeing the truth about whatever we are experiencing and tapping into the available resources more difficult. Eventually, we discover better ways of dealing with our challenges than resisting and complaining about them.

The biggest challenge in life comes from the ego. In its fear and ignorance, it harms others and suffers over every challenge. It even suffers over the good times. The ego wouldn't be happy even in heaven. And this dimension is definitely not heaven. It is designed for growth through adversity, so life provides exactly that.

If you said yes to everything life brings instead of no, as the ego does, you wouldn't suffer. Who you really are is in love with life and with every experience. And it's who you really are that has brought you the experiences you have had for your growth, or allowed you to create them by following the ego, also for your growth.

The gifts we are given to overcome adversity are the capacity to grow and learn from experience and the capacity to say yes to whatever is happening. Without those gifts, life on earth would be hell. But it isn't. It doesn't have to be if you discover within you that which loves it all.

What if you saw every person who comes into your life and every experience as exactly what you need? Who knows why that person or experience is in your life? But you can trust that that experience is good, not always easy perhaps, but always good. What if you really knew that it was all good? Everyone eventually discovers this. Why wait? Why not start believing this right now? The ego believes the opposite, and how has that been? When we align with something other than the ego, we discover that life is indeed good. Everything can bring us closer to love and to our true nature.

38: LET IT BE

In spiritual circles, we are often given the instruction to accept what is or let it be. That instruction is often confusing to spiritual seekers because, to the ego, it sounds passive. Accepting and allowing things to be implies a lack of action or involvement in changing what we may not like about something. But that's a misunderstanding. When we let whatever is be the way it is, we are simply accepting a fact of life—that whatever is, is the way it is. The truth is that we can't change whatever is. It's too late because it already is the way it is. Action can still be taken to change something, but it's useless to resist or complain about the way things already *are*.

The ego doesn't see it that way. It's rather determined to be unhappy with whatever is. The ego has very specific desires about each moment that are rarely met, so it withdraws from the moment into its ideas of what the moment *should* be or what it would like the moment to be. The ego doesn't give the present moment a chance to be experienced and appreciated for what it is.

"Let it be" counteracts the ego's tendency to reject what is and think *about* what is or about something else. Reminding ourselves to let it be can be a mantra, or affirmation, to neutralize the ego's rejection of the moment and help us become more present to life as it is showing up. Whenever you catch the ego in the act of rejecting whatever is, that's an opportunity to, instead, let it be by simply declaring it. That affirmation has the power to keep you in the present moment, in Essence.

It may seem far-fetched that a few words can be that powerful, but words are, in fact, what the ego uses to keep us identified with it. We can use words such as, "Let it be" to counteract the ego's voice in our head. When we use words this way, it is Essence using the mind to wake us up out of ego identification. What else would be doing this? Waking up happens when the *you* that has been asleep begins to detach from the illusion of itself as described by the mind and begins to experience itself as Essence. That is what's happening to many today. Many are waking up. What a wonder and a blessing!

39: BEING IN THE NOW IS NOT PASSIVE

The Now, the present moment, is a very alive place. It is always changing into something else. When we are in the Now and in our senses, what comes into our senses is constantly changing, isn't it? No moment is exactly like the last one or any other moment. The Now is a dynamic place, and actions and speech come out of it.

The ego conceives of the Now as static, however, which is one reason it rejects the Now. The ego doesn't value what the Now has to offer because the Now doesn't have what the ego wants: specialness. Instead, the sense of *me* and *my story* disappears when we drop into the Now. Dropping into the Now is an ego death of sorts (usually a very short one!), and the ego doesn't like that. It also doesn't like the Now because most moments aren't exciting enough for it. It wants life to be thrilling, like a rollercoaster ride, and it does what it can to make life that way. Sometimes it creates a ride you wish you could get off!

The ego imagines that if you meditate and live in the Now, you will never get anything done. It thinks you will be passive and sit around "contemplating our navel," and the ego can't see the value in that. What it doesn't understand is that sitting around doing nothing and feeling bad about doing nothing is a negative egoic state and not at all like meditating or being present in the moment.

Following the egoic mind often puts us into a lethargic or depressed state, where we feel unmotivated and unhappy. That unpleasant, passive state is the result of listening to the mind's discouragement, fear, discontentment, anger, and other negativity. Passivity also often results from the ego's contradictory desires or beliefs, which can cause us to feel stalemated. If you dropped into the Now and out of your head when you felt lethargic or depressed, you would find that Essence would move you to do something, and no matter how insignificant it might be, it would be fulfilling.

Lots of action comes out of the Now, but Essence also knows when rest is appropriate or meditating and listening within might be beneficial. Essence is alive in us in order to experience life through us, and that means doing things, expressing itself, creating, serving, learning, growing, and just plain enjoying life. When we are in Essence, we act, and our actions bring happiness and fulfillment, not only for ourselves, but for others. When we are identified with the ego, on the other hand, we often run around unnecessarily or engage in activities that are hurtful, selfish, counterproductive, or just unfulfilling. We follow one desire after another without ever finding satisfaction. That's the kind of action the ego engages in.

Life is very different, depending on where we live it from: the ego or Essence. The Now is anything but a passive place; it is where we overcome the passivity, boredom, stuckness, and lethargy of the ego and really begin to live life fully. When you allow yourself to remain in the Now long enough, you discover just how rich and alive it is. You also discover that you probably won't sit still for long! Essence has a lot it wants to do in life through each of us. It moves us to do and speak, but not through thought. When we live in the Now, our actions and speech flow out of the moment organically, spontaneously, simply, and meaningfully, and they feel just right.

40: AGING

Aging is one of the things the ego rails against because, to it, aging means loss—loss of beauty, strength, energy, and abilities. The ego doesn't see what is gained by aging, which is much more valuable than any of those other things. What is gained is wisdom, patience, understanding, compassion, and love. Isn't that like the ego to see only one side of things?

You might argue that not everyone becomes more wise, loving, and patient as they age. That would be true, at least perhaps in a particular lifetime. But as we evolve over many lifetimes, we do become wiser and more loving, and aging is one of the ways that happens. As we lose the things the ego loves, it is humbled, and the suffering motivates us to find other ways to be happy. When we get older, we need to discover how to be happy even when the ego doesn't have what it wants, and that's the great lesson of life!

Aging is relative, of course. Eighty year-olds refer to sixty year-olds as young, and they are, from that perspective. Aging is a matter of perspective, a matter of what we compare ourselves with. Most people suffer over aging because they compare themselves with their former, more youthful self, which they will never be again. What if you compared yourself, instead, to your future self? Then the self that you are now comes out looking pretty good! One simple way of overcoming the ego's suffering over aging is just to realize that you are as young right now as you will ever be! What a blessing.

Why waste time and energy—life—bemoaning the fact that you aren't what you were? The ego loves to do that. It loves to create problems, but aging isn't a problem the ego can solve. The ego's point of view only causes suffering. You can have that suffering, if you like, by taking the ego's point of view, or you can adopt the point of view of Essence, which loves life, including the miracle of aging and the opportunity for growth it provides.

Aging is the universal challenge: No one who lives long escapes it. As a result, a lot of wisdom about aging exists to draw upon. Unfortunately, some people never let go of their ego's perspective, and they suffer all the way to death. You don't have to. You can decide to be grateful for the life and body you have now, and you can choose to ignore anything else the ego has to say about getting older.

Those who suffer over aging usually spend a great deal of time and energy looking in the mirror, thinking about aging, and trying to do something about it. That is the ego's way of dealing with aging, and it can keep us very busy. It's fine if you want your life to be about that. However, you only have so much energy, and if you put it on your mind and its plans to try to be more beautiful and youthful, you won't have time and energy for other things that may be more meaningful.

What we put our attention on becomes our reality. Giving our looks and the aging process a lot of attention creates a particular experience of life, one that has considerable suffering, since going to battle with aging is a losing battle. But more importantly, dwelling on beauty and aging causes suffering because it's all about *me*. Focusing on the *me* and trying to improve it so that it's better than someone else or matches some ideal is inherently unfulfilling. What is fulfilling is loving, learning, growing, creating, serving others, developing and sharing our talents, and enjoying life, which is what happens when we forget about the *me*.

Whenever you focus on the *me*, you suffer. It's as simple as that. Aging can be an opportunity to finally give up that focus and give your attention to something more fulfilling. Focusing on the *me* is a stage of life. As we mature, we realize what makes for real happiness. That is the gift of aging, and it's the most precious realization. Then, aging stops mattering. You see that you never were the *me* that worried so much about what you looked like anyway. What a wonderful discovery! You are free to just live, without having to cater to the *me* anymore.

41: THE INTERDEPENDENCE OF ALL THINGS

Each of us is entirely unique, and that uniqueness serves Creation. Because of that uniqueness, everyone is equally valuable. Everyone has their part to play, and everyone's part is needed. Everyone has a life purpose, but no one's life purpose is more important than another's because everyone needs everyone else to exist and do their life purpose. The President of the United States, or anyone else we might assume has an important life purpose, couldn't do what he or she does without food and other necessities. Without someone making and shipping the computers, automobiles, and other supplies, and picking up the garbage and doing all the other necessary tasks, businesses and families couldn't survive. Everyone depends on everyone else for all the goods and services they need and to be able to do what they do.

When we contemplate our interdependence and our interconnectedness with everything, we realize what a marvelous and amazing Intelligence must be behind it all to provide so well for itself, for the Whole. How amazingly well everything functions to support the Whole! Yes, there are times when functioning breaks down, but even that is only temporary before a rebalancing occurs. Periodically, a natural breaking down and reorganization happens, which isn't wrong or bad, as the ego might see it, but a normal part of the evolution of humanity and society. Even when a breakdown occurs as a result of negative choices, such as war, an eventual rebalancing occurs and, moreover, learning that will hopefully prevent such choices from being made again.

Once you recognize how well you are taken care of within existence, you can begin to trust life more. The ego has a tendency to focus on what it feels is lacking and what it wants more of, but the truth is you are existing just fine right now. Life has supported you so far—you are here. It's important to acknowledge the many ways that life (through others, your own efforts, and society) has taken care of you, especially when you are feeling afraid or unsupported.

The ego naturally fears life. It doesn't recognize the interconnectedness of all life. It feels separate and alone, which is where the fear comes from. The truth is, however, we aren't separate and alone, but part of a larger Whole within which each of us functions. The Whole adjusts itself to take care of all that exists within it. Sometimes the adjustments take a while, but support eventually manifests as needed. It's possible to learn to trust that completely instead of trusting the ego's fears and worries. When you begin to trust that the Whole takes care of itself—takes care us—you discover just how trustworthy life is. But that is the catch, isn't it? It does take somewhat of a leap of faith.

The other option, distrusting life, has its cost, however. When we distrust life, we often make choices that aren't aligned with life. For example, we might choose security, which is a favorite choice of the ego, over what makes our Heart sing, and then end up unhappy. Fortunately, life has a built-in correction mechanism: suffering. Not being happy motivates us to find a way to be happy.

We are meant to be happy and to do what makes us happy. We discover what makes us happy by following our joy instead of doing what makes us unhappy. This is a simple enough prescription. The only thing that can interfere with following that prescription for happiness is fear. Fortunately, fear is just a negative thought about the future that has no validity or value. So there is no reason to follow fear instead of your Heart and every reason to.

42: DESIRE

Desires drive life. We assume that getting what we want will make us happy, but do you really know that it will? One way to find out is to ask yourself if getting what you wanted in the past has ever made you happy for long. Everyone gets what they want some of the time. Has getting what you wanted made you happy? For how long?

When people say they want to be happy, they usually mean they want to have a certain feeling about life. They want to feel glad to be alive, exuberant, loving, generous, and good about themselves and others. Is that what you get when you get what you want?

The next time you get what you want, really notice what happens. What you are likely to experience when you get what you want is a surge of *feelings:* excitement, pleasure, happiness, relaxation, and relief. At last, you have arrived, you can relax, you get to stop striving, you get to feel good about yourself. Feelings of relaxation, elation, and relief come from the cessation of the ego's pushing, striving, doubting, fears, and tension around what it desired. What a relief it is when all that striving and tension finally stop!

Our desires create a state of tension that underlies our experience of life to some degree until that desire is met. That state of tension is quite unpleasant; it's certainly not a state of happiness. Desiring something is uncomfortable, and the only relief seems to be in attaining what we want. The discomfort of desiring makes getting what we want all the more pressing. As a result, what we desire takes on much more importance. Now, we feel we really do need that to be happy, to end the torment of desiring. The *belief* that we need something to be happy causes great unhappiness, and the resulting tension begs to be resolved.

Once we've gotten what we wanted, the feeling of relief and happiness is real. That kind of happiness is a feeling. All feelings come and go, and so does that kind of happiness, sometimes very quickly. There's another kind of happiness—true happiness—that isn't a feeling, but our natural state. True happiness doesn't come and go, and it doesn't come from getting what we want, but in loving what we've got, which is something we can always do. We can always love what we've got! So true happiness is always available. We experience it when we are in touch with our true nature.

The natural state is usually obscured by the ego's discontentment. When that discontentment disappears or is ignored, true happiness is revealed, but it was always there. That's the happiness we can count on, and we don't have to strive to get or achieve something to experience it. It is the happiness you have been looking for all along that was never found in getting and achieving.

Why be tense, discontent, and unhappy over trying to get or achieve something so that you can be happy, when getting what you really want requires only that you not do that? The ego is afraid that if its desires aren't pursued, nothing will be gotten or accomplished and happiness will be out of reach, and it convinces us of that. But that simply isn't true. Essence is active in our life, and it moves us to pursue what we need to be supported and fulfilled, and it brings us what we need to be supported and fulfilled. Essence is much wiser than the ego, so why follow the false master, who only makes you miserable?

Doing what makes us miserable is not what Essence asks of us. Being miserable is the ego's creation. Essence asks only that we follow what brings us joy and that we trust that the rest will fall into place. Getting what the ego wants doesn't bring us joy. We assume it will, but it doesn't. At best, it brings fleeting relief from the misery of the ego. Life doesn't have to be about trying to get our desires met. Instead, it can be about meeting whatever is showing up right now and loving it, and discovering in each moment where life wants to take us.

43: SPONTANEITY VS. CONDITIONING

Spontaneity is a sign of being in Essence. When we are in Essence, the experience is one of being in the flow, and we respond naturally and spontaneously to life. This is very different from automatically and unconsciously reacting to our conditioning. The way that the spontaneity of Essence and our automatic conditioned responses are alike is that both result it action that isn't thought about or evaluated ahead of time. However, the results of these two ways of being are very different, and the experience is very different too.

Responding to Essence's urges, drives, and inspiration feels natural, easy. Such responses flow organically out of the moment, and the results feel good. The results of our automatic conditioned responses, on the other hand, don't feel good. Acting out our conditioning leaves us contracted and also often leaves others contracted.

If you pay close attention to how you are feeling moment to moment, it's not hard at all to tell the difference between automatic action in response to the ego and automatic action in response to Essence. Once you have this level of awareness, it's possible to become conscious of what was formerly unconscious and to become free of acting out your conditioning. This is an amazing step—to consciously choose our response to life rather than react to life from our conditioning, which leaves everyone feeling bad.

When we become more aware of our conditioning, we are less at the mercy of it. A space develops between our thoughts and actions, which allows us to choose our actions rather than react unconsciously. Often our immediate reactions and responses are conditioned ones. If we can hold off from reacting automatically to our conditioning, we can discover another way of being in the world, one that is wiser and based on love and compassion for others.

When egos are coming at us, we often respond from our ego. Rather than taking the path of least resistance and responding from the ego, if you just say no to that initial response and allow yourself to see how Essence is moving you instead, you can discover a wiser and gentler way of being with others and with life. If you can put off your conditioned tendencies for just a bit, Essence will move you to speak and act,. Then it's possible to get to know the being that you really are and how this being moves in life.

44: THE DIFFERENCE BETWEEN INSIGHT AND JUDGMENT

Insight is a wonderful thing. It comes from Essence. Judgment is not a wonderful thing, and it comes from the ego, without exception. These two things, insight and judgment, often follow one after the other: Insight turns into judgment. The ego often co-opts insights that arise from Essence. It takes a lot of diligence to not fall into the trap of ego-inflation because we suddenly realize something we hadn't realized before. A natural elation arises when we have an insight, and then the ego comes in and takes credit for that insight and often turns it into a judgment.

Because it's much easier to see someone else's weaknesses than our own, we receive insights about others more easily than about ourselves. An insight about someone else is helpful when it leads to acceptance (e.g., "He's impulsive, but I love him anyway"), but not helpful when it leads to a judgment that's either kept to ourselves or shared with that person or with others. When an insight results in acceptance, that is Essence; when it results in judgment, that is the ego.

No matter how wonderful an insight is, if it's held as a judgment within us, it's likely to harm our relationship with the person that it's about. And if that judgment that is disguised as an insight is shared, it's likely to be harmful as well. Even when the intent in sharing it is to help someone, doing so is likely to be harmful to our relationship with that person because he or she hasn't asked for that insight. Insight that hasn't been asked for is often received as criticism, and most people don't or can't make use of criticism because it activates their egos and causes them to become defensive or angry and judgmental in return. Criticism and judgment have no place in relationships. Whether we are holding a judgment or receiving one, judgments hurt.

The ego often tries to convince us to share our judgments by telling us that it would be helpful to share them, but it rarely is. That is the pretense the ego uses to perpetuate its superiority game. Judgment is the weapon the ego uses to prove that it's right and superior and someone else isn't. This isn't a game that feels good to anyone, and relationships can't survive for very long when this game is going on. Some relationships don't survive even one bout of judgment.

Insights are given to us by Essence to heal us, evolve us, and point the way to greater love and wisdom. They can do that, or they can be harmful if they turn into a judgment. Seeing the mechanism by which the ego twists insights into a negative force will help you avoid this pitfall and use your insights for good.

45: COMPASSION IS NOT A THOUGHT OR FEELING

When someone we know is going through something difficult, we often feel we have to think about their situation, worry about it, tell people about it, complain about it, be angry or afraid about it, or even cry about it. That is the ego's version of compassion. However, that really isn't compassion, but rather sympathy. One of the definitions of "sympathy" is: "a relationship or an affinity between people or things in which whatever affects one correspondingly affects the other." (The American Heritage Dictionary of the English Language, Fourth Edition, 2000, Houghton Mifflin Company.)

Sympathy is the ego's version of compassion, but sympathy is a poor substitute for compassion. Suffering over someone else's suffering isn't actually compassionate. It puts the sympathetic person in the same boat with the person who is having difficulty, and that makes the sympathetic person less likely to be of help. The sympathetic ego joins the other person in his or her suffering, and that reinforces the ego's view that whatever happened or is happening is terrible and shouldn't be the way it is.

The perspective that something shouldn't be the way it is, is untrue (reality is the way it is) and not helpful. If something *is*, then asserting that it shouldn't be just keeps us stuck in anger and sadness, and those feelings don't help us through challenging times. And as unpleasant or unfortunate as something might be, asserting that it's terrible and focusing on that only reinforces and maintains the experience of it being terrible. No matter how difficult something is, it is always possible to tap in to Essence's acceptance and the support it has to offer. The ego sees things in black and white: terrible and wonderful. But life is more complex than that. Every experience is "a mixed bag."

Acceptance and healing come from moving out of the ego's limited, black and white point of view into a more complete view—Essence's view. When we are experiencing difficulties, we need Essence's perspective, the perspective that "this too shall pass" and that whatever is being experienced can serve our growth and be used for good.

Our experiences can make us more loving and wise, and they are often designed to do that. Or we can take the ego's low road of anger, resentment, hatred, sadness, and fear, but doing that won't take us where we want to go. Acceptance is the key that unlocks the door to Essence. In difficult times, we are particularly challenged to accept whatever life has brought us. Such times, in fact, often teach us acceptance because the alternative is unbearable.

The compassionate response to those going through difficulties isn't to agree with a perspective that increases their suffering, but to offer them a truer, less limiting perspective, one that will help them connect with Essence and grow as a result of their challenges. To do that, we have to be aligned with the compassion and wisdom of Essence, not the sympathy of the ego.

46: PATIENCE

Patience is the absence of impatience, which is a common experience when we are identified with the ego. If we are feeling impatient, we are identified with the ego and some conditioned idea. Impatience is usually fueled by the desire for something else to be happening, to be in a more ideal, future moment rather than the present moment. The ego feels that way most of the time to some extent. It's almost always looking forward to something better, something more in keeping with its desires and fantasies. The present moment falls short, so the ego longs for something better.

All this suffering is unnecessary because the truth is that the moment never falls short except in the ego's (our) imagination. How can it? Fall short of what? An idea? How real is an idea? How can the moment be anything but what it is, and how can that be bad? Only if we declare it so. What declares this? The ego. Why? Because it is programmed to find fault and generate problems.

When we experience life without giving our experience a mental interpretation—a spin—life is just as it is. Spin wouldn't be so bad if what was doing the spinning wasn't so negative, but the ego puts a negative spin on life. It rejects life, and that rejection creates feelings: fear, impatience, anger, victimization, shame, hurt, guilt, jealousy, sadness, envy, or resentment. Negative feelings come from the ego's negative interpretations of life. Fear, for example, is the result of the negative spin given to a moment in the future (which doesn't even exist!).

Once our feelings have been triggered, the ego's story seems really true. After all, look how that situation made you feel! We are programmed to believe our feelings—our feelings can't be wrong! We believe that our feelings give us accurate information about our experience. But instead of reflecting the truth about an experience, our feelings reflect the spin put on that experience by the ego. We feel the way we do because of our thoughts about it, not because the situation, itself, made us feel that way.

The way to dissolve and move beyond those negative feelings is simply to see that a story about the situation, not the situation, created those feelings. If you feel impatient, how did you create that feeling? What did you tell yourself that caused you to feel that way? Also notice how you imagined yourself having a better moment, and notice how that made you feel. That only fueled the flames, right? What if you had just let the moment be as it was without deciding it came up short and without imagining something better? What if you hadn't believed your thoughts about the experience you were having? It would have been a very different experience.

How we experience life is our choice. We are meant to discover the power we have to agree with certain thoughts or not. You can have the experience the mind tells you to have and all the feelings that go with that, or you can just experience the experience, which simply requires openness and curiosity: "Oh this, yes this, and this too. Interesting. And now what?"

That curiosity doesn't detach us from life. Instead, it allows us to fully and purely experience life and respond naturally and spontaneously without our thoughts and conditioning intervening and interfering. It seems like our thoughts and conditioning are useful, but they only get in the way of love, happiness, peace, and wisdom. You can live without them. When you do, you will still use the functional aspect of your mind when you need it, but you know the egoic mind has nothing for you. What freedom!

47: BELIEVING

Have you noticed that believing something doesn't make it so? As much as the ego would like to think that believing something has the power to make it happen, belief just doesn't have that much power. You have believed lots of things that never came to pass, and many things have come to pass that you never believed would happen. The ego wants so much to be able to control life so that it can get what it wants, but the purpose of life isn't to please the ego. This egocentric view is, in fact, the cause of so much suffering. The ego wants life its way, but life isn't about giving the ego what it wants, but about pointing us to what brings lasting happiness and fulfillment: love, peace, unity, goodness, compassion, wisdom, service, learning, and growth.

Belief does have some power, however. A positive belief has the power to neutralize a negative one, and negative beliefs can stop us from taking action that might bring us what we want. That is why believing something positive often has the effect of creating it. Positive beliefs don't cause what we want to happen, however, as much as they allow what we want to be created or received by us because we aren't blocking it by thinking negatively. Affirmations work, not because the affirmation itself creates what we want, but because an affirmation can help us release, or neutralize, any beliefs that stand in the way of creating or receiving what we want.

Our negative beliefs are powerful if we believe them. But if we don't, they have no power whatsoever. Can an idea affect the world? Only if it's believed and only if it's put into action. The belief itself, which is just an idea, has no power of its own. Everyone has beliefs and negative thoughts. If they aren't believed, they end there and quickly disappear. They may show up again and again, but if they are ignored, they don't affect us or anything else.

We don't have the power to determine what thoughts show up in our mind, but we do have the power to choose to believe them and respond to them or not. Not everyone realizes they have that power, but that doesn't mean they don't. What an amazing step in evolution it is to realize you have this power. That realization is the beginning of freedom from the egoic mind.

When negative thoughts have been reinforced repeatedly by believing them, you may not feel like you have much power to ignore them. Thoughts that have been believed and reinforced by feelings and actions can feel very compelling, but you always have the choice to give them your attention or not. That power to choose is the great gift we have been given. But we have to use that gift, and that sometimes takes considerable will. When you first begin to choose differently, ignoring a thought instead of believing it can seem very difficult—almost impossible. But each subsequent choice becomes easier.

Eventually, those negative thoughts won't show up anymore, and a choice won't even be necessary. You will function from Essence, and the egoic mind will be like a whisper in the background, if you experience it at all. Waking up isn't easy. For most people, it is a gradual process that requires choosing over and over again not to listen to the negative mind but to something else that speaks to us and moves us, not through our mind, but through our intuition and our very being.

48: FEAR IS JUST A THOUGHT

Fear is what keeps people identified with the ego. It keeps people hostage to the suffering inherent in the human condition, but it doesn't have to be that way. Fear is the most powerful tool the ego has, but fear is just a thought. And how powerful is a thought, really? If we don't believe a thought, it has no power whatsoever. Fear is only powerful if we believe it, and it has absolutely no other ability to affect reality.

The catch is that fear is so believable. A fearful thought, which is a thought about the future, gets cloaked in emotions, and those emotions are felt in the body, making the fear seem very real. We interpret that feeling as meaningful: If a thought makes us feel that way, we assume that thought must be meaningful. We think there must be something true about it, so we believe it and give it the power to affect our life. The truth is a fearful thought isn't any more real than any other thought. Our fears don't predict the future—they aren't premonitions of what will be. They also don't protect us from what we fear.

When we examine this, we see that we hold a superstitious belief in our fears. We are programmed to have fearful thoughts and believe them, but that doesn't make those thoughts true! What if you really knew that none of your fears were true or had value? You would be free of them! So whenever a fearful thought arises, notice that thought, note that it's a fearful thought, and then remind yourself that it's meaningless and untrue.

If you are grabbed by the *emotion* of fear, notice that feeling, accept that it is here, and sit with that feeling with curiosity and acceptance until it reveals the thoughts that are behind it.

Discovering the beliefs behind a fear and then recognizing that those beliefs are false can free us from this same fear returning.

Fears are problematic not only because they are unpleasant and cause us to suffer, but also because they can cause us to make choices that aren't aligned with Essence. Fears come from the ego—not Essence—and they serve the ego. So when we follow our fears, we are following the ego, and the ego doesn't know what will make us happy and fulfilled. Fears are also problematic because they drive wars and other atrocities on this planet. So if you want peace and love in your life, start by not giving any attention to your fearful thoughts or the fears of others.

49: TREATS

Many of us were conditioned as children to expect rewards for good behavior, such as studying or eating all our dinner. So now, when we are faced with having to do something we don't want to do, we may turn to a treat to get us through it or make it more palatable. As the song says, "A spoonful of sugar helps the medicine go down."

For most people, treats as children came in the form of cookies or other sweets. Thus, being good, doing good, and being deserving became associated with sweets. As a result, sweets also became a way of trying to feel good about ourselves: When our parents felt good about us, they gave us sweets, so if we give ourselves sweets, we will feel good about ourselves (hopefully). That is the logic, or illogic, behind this.

On a very basic level, eating sweets or some other treat food does provide some relief, simply because we believe it does. For a moment, you feel like you did as a child: relaxed, happy, and at ease with yourself. The problem is those feelings last only very briefly, if at all. You still have the essential problem of not liking something about life or yourself. Until that issue is addressed, treats are a temporary band-aid. They become a coping mechanism for dealing with the ego's discontentment. Since the ego is discontent so much of the time, this coping mechanism may be called on a lot, and the result is often a dysfunctional relationship with food.

Being at the mercy of our conditioning never feels good. We feel out of control, and that makes it difficult to feel good about ourselves, which often leads to seeking more comfort from food.

For many people, this is quite a vicious cycle: Trying to feel good leads to treating ourselves, which leads to not feeling good about ourselves, which leads to more eating. The problem is treating ourselves with food is an ineffective coping mechanism. The ego doesn't have any good coping mechanisms for dealing with the stress and discontentment it creates. It drives us to eat, drink, do drugs, shop, or indulge in other compulsive or escapist behaviors.

The only way out of this vicious cycle is to drop all coping mechanisms and get to the root of the issue, which is the ego's discontentment with and resistance to life. The ego resists life automatically, and it creates discontentment by imagining, dreaming, and wanting life to be different. Once you realize that the resistance to life and even the fantasies and desires are not *yours*, but the ego's, you can become free of the ego's discontentment. To be free, you notice the thoughts that demand that life be different and pleasing to the ego, and you see that the ego is like a child throwing a tantrum. Moreover, you see that you are not the ego.

The ego doesn't exist as a thing or entity, but it seems to exist and is part of our unconscious. We are the spaciousness that's experiencing that phenomenon and everything else in life. That spaciousness is totally at ease with life, even with the ego being the way it is. The tension and stress belong to the ego, not to the spaciousness. So when we are identified with the spaciousness and not the ego, there's no sense of needing to cope with life. Life isn't a problem to be coped with.

Happiness is a choice. It's the choice to not listen to the childish, self-centered aspect of ourselves, but to pay attention, instead, to life as it is showing up right now, without our stories about how we'd like it to be showing up. Being here in the present moment is always delightful if we don't allow ourselves to be distracted by the ego's discontentment. The ego chatters on, and you just stay here in the moment, where it's possible to feel Essence's joy in being alive.

50: TRUSTING LIFE

Trust is the antidote to fear and therefore immensely important to bringing more peace and love to this beautiful earth. What we can trust is the goodness behind all life, the goodness within us, which chooses love over hatred and peace over conflict. What we really are is goodness, but it's covered over by identification with the ego, or that part of us that feels fearful, distrusting, and alone. When we drop out of ego identification, we discover the "peace that passeth all understanding." From that place of inner peace, world peace is truly possible.

What we can't trust is the very thing that makes us distrust Essence (our essential goodness), and that's the ego. How ironic! The ego causes us to distrust what's truly trustworthy, and that leaves us trusting the ego, which is untrustworthy! This is quite a setup. This challenge is part of the design of life, and it was designed this way to offer a challenge—the challenge of overcoming fear. If we can do that, we win the greatest prize: love, peace, contentment, and joy. Are you willing to give up your fear for love, peace, contentment, and joy? Are you willing to trust something other than the ego? How has it been for you to trust the ego? Has it brought you love, peace, contentment, and joy?

Trusting the ego brings the opposite of peace. It brings only discontentment. When we listen to the egoic mind, we feel discontent, fearful, and distrusting. The only way out of those feelings is to see that there's something else besides the ego, and that's Essence, our essential goodness. Essence co-creates our life with the ego. It brings us the experiences we need to grow and evolve toward love. And it allows us to create experiences by following our ego, because we grow from those experiences too.

Life is a dance between the ego and Essence. The more we let Essence lead this dance, the more smoothly life will go.

The ego isn't trustworthy because it doesn't have the capacity to understand life and the immensity of the Intelligence that's behind life. It doesn't see the big picture and doesn't know where the flow is going. The ego guides us according to its values and desires, which are related to getting more power, security, wealth, superiority, and safety. There's nothing wrong with these things, but so much is left out! Life is about so much more, especially love, and the ego knows nothing about love.

The ego is the opponent of love. To experience more love, peace, and happiness requires overcoming the fears and distrust of the ego and learning to trust life, the goodness within us. What we are—goodness—is living our life perfectly and is perfectly trustworthy. Life is good. Can you trust that? What's the alternative?

51: YOU DON'T NEED TO HAVE NOTHING TO DO TO DO NOTHING

In the midst of our busy lives, we often don't just stop and do nothing—relax and just be. When we are caught up in busy-ness, taking a break seems unreasonable. But that's probably when taking a break would be most beneficial. The ego will push and push us to do more and accomplish more if we keep giving in to it. The more we do, the more the ego comes up with to do. This busy-ness becomes a lifestyle, and then we can't even imagine what life would be like if we didn't have so much to do.

This kind of lifestyle is pretty much the norm in the United States, so we may not even question it. The trouble with all this doing is that the ego is often running this running around: "Do this. You have to do this. Don't forget to do that. When you're done with that...." And this becomes what our life is about. If you wait for the demands that the ego makes on your time and energy to end before you take time out to do nothing, your time-outs will be few and far between.

When you are rushing, doing, going, pushing, you are in the grip of the ego. Are you enjoying yourself? That's the test, really, of whether the ego is running you or not. If you are busy and "in joy," that's quite different than if you are at the mercy of The Tyrant, the ego that pushes us to do more and more and do it more perfectly and faster than is even humanly possible. Let joy and enjoyment be your guide to whether you keep doing something or stop and take a break.

When you aren't experiencing joy in what you are doing, stop, take a break, and discover what you need in order to regain that sense of joy. Don't waste another moment of this precious life pushing yourself through life. Take a break from the ego's ideas of how to live your life and discover how Essence would move you if you gave it a chance to. It might not move you at all, or it might move you in a different direction. A lack of joy is a sign that you are out of alignment with this that is living you, because Essence feels joy in moving through life. Essence can show you how to move through life more joyfully. Follow Essence's lead, its pushes, instead of the ego's.

How do you discover how Essence would move you? By stopping and doing nothing and listening inside, by being here, now, in this moment without the mind's check-list and ideas about life. Just for a moment, let yourself be here in life, as if it were your last hour, with no future, no past, just this, now. How is it to just be? Let the feeling of just being sink in for as long as you need to in order to shift gears from doing to being.

Being is a very rich place. The ego calls being "doing nothing," but being is experiencing the moment just as it is. Out of just being arises your "marching orders," the ones that are meaningful and necessary to you, the ones from Essence. From just being, you will be naturally moved to do whatever you need to do, and you will be moved to rest when that's appropriate. When we push ourselves unnecessarily, we fall out of alignment with our Being, which is capable of running our life much more smoothly than the ego—and with joy. You don't have to give up joy to "have a life." Joy is meant to be part of life. Taking time to do nothing in the midst of the busy-ness of life is the way back to joy.

Does this sound too simple? That would be the egoic mind's take on this great truth. The Truth is too simple for the mind. The ego turns away from the Truth. Happiness is more available than you may realize. It isn't found in doing and accomplishing, except briefly, because we're never done doing and accomplishing. Happiness is found in fully experiencing life while we are doing or not doing. It's found in being fully present to whatever we are doing or whatever is happening. If you aren't experiencing joy in doing something, then stop, reconnect with your joy, and bring that new-found joy into what you are doing.

52: THE FIRST RESPONSE

The first and automatic response to anything, such as a request from someone or even an opportunity, is likely to come from the ego. We are programmed to respond automatically, and this programming is released into the mind as a thought, opinion, belief, point of view, attitude, or emotional reaction. Often the response is similar to how we have responded many times before, and it usually has some psychological, emotional, or even astrological basis.

Notice how quickly you come up with a response to something or someone, such as someone asking you to do something. If a response isn't quick, it's usually because of conflicting programming: Two different programmed responses are in conflict, in which case, the immediate reaction might be confusion, frustration, or anger.

If you identify with the first response, that is, if you take the egoic mind's voice as *your* voice, *your* opinion, or *your* reaction, chances are that response won't be very charitable or wise because the ego isn't either of these. When you give voice to the ego, you won't feel very good about yourself because the ego's responses tend to be self-centered, unkind, and narrow-minded, which is how we feel when we are identified with the ego.

When that happens, you might try to feel better about yourself through various strategies. You might try to build a case to justify your responses, and judgments are often part of that. Since judging never feels good, the ego may try to feel better by seeking pleasure or in other ways trying to improve its self-image or situation, all because you bought into your initial, automatic reaction.

Once you realize that your initial reaction is most likely from the ego, you can just wait a moment for some other reaction to arise from deeper within you, from Essence. If Essence is given a chance, it will act and speak through you. But if you act and speak automatically from the ego, you won't discover how Essence might have responded.

You can tell when Essence is speaking and acting through you because instead of being tense, confused, or unkind, you feel at peace, open, accepting, and loving. Your response to a request, for instance, may still be no, but you will deliver that "no" in a way that the person won't feel hurt or offended.

As we mature, we usually do learn to be kinder because acting out of the ego gets us into trouble. Egos aren't very nice, and most of us learn to be nice by holding back our initial reactions. Doing that is certainly better than giving voice to an unkind ego, but that can leave us with negative feelings if we still believe our ego's viewpoint. The way out of these feelings is to recognize that those thoughts are the ego's and not your true voice. Don't agree with the egoic mind, stay apart from it, and just notice it. Then you can discover your true voice.

You don't have to *try* to be nice; you only have to realize that what isn't nice about you (and everyone else) is the ego, and not who you really are. Step back and give some space and time to your initial thoughts and reactions, and you will discover Essence, which has the wisdom and love to bring peace and harmony to any situation.

53: HOW'S IT GOING?

When we run into someone, we often greet him or her with, "How's it going?" That question reflects the ongoing concern of the ego about its own world: "How's it going *for me?*" Have you noticed just how present that question is in your mind throughout your day? The ego is constantly checking: "How's it going for me?" The ego evaluates each event, experience, act, and encounter to determine how that enhances or detracts from what the ego is trying to create: "Will that help get me what I want or not?"

The ego has an agenda, and what happens is seen as either advancing that agenda or not. It might be as simple as, "I have to be successful" or "I have to get married and have children." What is your ego's agenda? What is it trying to get or where is it trying to go? This agenda is also called a *story* in spiritual circles. The ego has a story about how the past has gone, how the present is going, and how the future is supposed to go. How it's supposed to go is the ego's agenda.

Stories are ideas the ego brings *to* life, which shape our perceptions, create feelings, and even drive actions, but nonetheless don't relate to what is happening in the moment. When what's going on fits your story, you (if you are identified with the ego) relax and feel happy; and when it doesn't, you feel stressed and unhappy. The ego doesn't consider that its story is the problem. The ego just wants what it wants, and it thinks life should provide that. It doesn't see that its demands on life are what cause its unhappiness and discontentment. The story seems so real and true, so how can it be the problem? The ego figures there must be some way to make life fit its story, its agenda. And the ego works very hard to do that. All the while, life has its own agenda. Life unfolds in its own way, irrespective of the story and the desires that drive the story.

The story doesn't create life, and it doesn't even help us create life. It only creates dissatisfaction with life and ourselves because we will never be able to make life conform to our story. If you believe you should be able to, you will feel bad about yourself. Yes, life does conform to our story sometimes. How wonderful! But that doesn't mean we can or should be able to get it to conform always. No one has ever succeeded in creating their reality just the way they wanted it. That's because life isn't about getting what we want, but about something much deeper and more meaningful. It's about life creating in all sorts of ways, life evolving, and life serving life.

We are part of the Whole and function within that, and it has an intention for our life and the lives of others. When we are aligned with the Whole, we feel happy; when we aren't, we feel empty and unfulfilled. Following the ego's agenda won't bring you fulfillment, although it will bring you lots of experiences. You can follow the ego's agenda, or you can fall in love with whatever is happening. When you fall in love with what is, you discover that life unfolds beautifully, purposefully, and happily without the ego's stories and agendas.

54: ENJOY WHATEVER YOU ARE DOING

Whatever you are doing, enjoy it! You have another option, of course, which is to not enjoy it. Notice what keeps you from enjoying whatever you are doing. It's your thoughts, isn't it? Even when you are experiencing pain or something unpleasant, like going to the dentist, if you don't listen to any negative thoughts, fears, complaints, and desires about it, you won't suffer. You'll just have the experience.

Our thoughts about whatever we are doing interfere with enjoying it not only because they are often negative, judgmental, or resistant to the experience, but also because thoughts—even positive ones—remove us from an experience to some degree. Some thoughts don't interfere much with being present and enjoying what we are doing; they just float in and out of our mind, without taking very much of our attention. Other thoughts, however, grab us, and we lose touch with what we are doing and the experience we are having. When that happens, it feels like we are going through the motions or doing something just to get it done.

We can go through life this way if we want, but when we aren't fully in contact with what we're doing, we miss out on the potential joy and pleasure in it. Any experience can be interesting, since we have never had it before. And any experience can be enjoyed, because when we are immersed in it, we lose the false self (the sense of I or me) and discover our true self, which is always enjoying life. Essence is always in-joy. And from Essence's standpoint, every moment is an opportunity to serve life and love, which is another source of joy. What if you approached each moment as an opportunity to experience, serve, or love?

The secret to enjoying whatever you are doing is getting lost in it, getting involved in it. That means getting all your senses involved in it or, more accurately, noticing how all your senses *are* involved in it. Noticing sensory experience takes us out of our egoic mind (our functional mind is still available) and into the experience we are having. When you are present to the experience you are having, you are in the moment, where it's possible to experience Presence, or Essence. The experience of Essence is highly pleasurable, so no matter what you are doing, if you are present to it, it will be enjoyable.

What's so hard about being present? It takes some practice to be in our body and aware of our sensory experience because the habit of being absorbed in thought is so deeply ingrained. We have to practice being present again and again to neutralize the old habit of identifying with our mind, and that takes dedication and commitment.

Meditation is a way of practicing being present, and it will really help you live in the moment more. Meditation teaches us to detach from the egoic mind, observe it, and see it for what it is. Objectivity toward the mind is essential in breaking the programming that causes us to identify with it. You can even learn to enjoy meditation if you don't listen to the mind's resistance to it!

55: COMMITMENT

When you make a choice to do something, commit yourself to it while you are doing it. What so often happens is that people make a choice to do something and then they don't fully commit to it— they don't fully say yes to it while they are doing it. They might complain about doing it, dream about doing something else, or not invest themselves in it, all the while they are doing it. The ego tends to resist and distance itself even from what it chooses to do.

And once something is chosen, the ego often keeps people in situations they aren't happy with by making it difficult for them to see their way out. It keeps them from making a different choice by either confusing them with too many options or shooting down every option that comes along. On the other hand, the ego might suggest making changes constantly as a way of trying to be happy. The ego doesn't know when to stay and when to go! That's the truth.

Listening to the egoic mind will make you miserable, whether or not a choice is the right one from the standpoint of Essence. The mind questions our choices and brings dissatisfaction into every moment. Even when we are aligned with Essence's intentions, the mind often complains, doubts, questions, and judges because that's what the mind does. When that's happening, being true to our choice, even when it's the right one, may be challenging. The mind will make you miserable in the midst of any choice if you let it.

By the way, many choices are perfectly fine with Essence because we learn from everything we do. There isn't necessarily one "right" choice, but almost always many possible paths to take that would be satisfying and fulfill Essence's intentions. However, some choices clearly won't be aligned with Essence, and those are bound to not be fulfilling or make us happy, although we might learn a great deal from them! Essence works hard to steer us toward what will be fulfilling and away from what won't be.

The ego, which operates through our thoughts, doesn't know what will fulfill us, and when we are doing what could fulfill us, the ego doesn't necessarily realize that and may sabotage it. This is challenging but less so when we recognize that thoughts don't have the answer to what to do. Only the silent, subtle wisdom that comes from the Heart (Essence), which is *felt* and intuited rather than thought, can be trusted to have the answer.

Making a choice and then not fully involving ourselves in what we have chosen makes no sense and only creates suffering. But when we listen to the egoic mind, that's often what happens. You may have the perfect job or relationship for you—the one designed and brought to you by Essence—and you may not realize it and feel discontent and restless.

On the other hand, restlessness or depression may be a sign of not being aligned with Essence. These feelings may be messages from Essence that you need to make a different choice. When that's the case, those feelings will come from deep within you and not from a thought. They won't manifest as complaints and judgments, but as a sense that something isn't right for you. You might put that sense of something not being right into words and express it as a complaint, and that might create emotions, so this can make for confusion.

Although this is a little tricky, with some examination and discrimination between thoughts and intuitive feelings, you can determine for yourself what's true. Then when you make a choice, be sure to say yes to it as long as you are choosing that. Jump into whatever you have chosen to do or whomever you have chosen to be with, with both feet and do it with all your Heart. If and when the time comes to jump out, if you are attuned to your intuition, you will know when to make a different choice.

56: BE KIND TO YOURSELF

Love is the underlying fabric of life, and kindness is its reflection in the world, through us. It can be conveyed in attentiveness to others, in words, or in deeds. One of the most powerful acts of kindness is kindness toward ourselves. That is really where kindness begins. If we aren't kind to ourselves, how can we be kind to others? Unless we are also kind to ourselves, kindness toward others is more of a manipulation, an attempt to get others to give us something, including love. However, unless we are kind to ourselves, we won't even be able to take in any kindness we do receive from others. That place of lack inside of us can't be filled from the outside. First, we have to be kind to ourselves.

True kindness comes from a desire to soothe and comfort others because we have discovered the power and blessing of kindness as a result of having received it. Receiving kindness from others heals us and makes it possible to express it to others. If we haven't received much kindness from others, we need to find a way to give it to ourselves, to be kind to ourselves even though others may not have been. To do that, we have to do two things: We have to forgive those who weren't kind to us, and we have to see that we deserve love.

Unfortunately, those who didn't receive a lot of kindness as children usually concluded that they deserved that and that they aren't lovable. They need to forgive those who were unable to be kind to them (probably because they were treated the same way when they were young) and learn to give love to themselves. Those who were abused learned to abuse themselves inwardly; they learned to believe their negative thoughts about themselves. They need to develop a loving inner voice rather than an unloving one.

That can be done, but it takes a willingness to see the truth, to see through the negative self-image to the truth—that you are divinity in a human body, that you are love incarnate.

Everyone has the same capacity to love, but that ability may have been squelched by not having been loved. Not being loved as a child blocks the natural flow of love, and giving love to yourself allows love to flow outward again. It's always possible to give ourselves love because our true nature (Essence) loves the human expression that we are, no matter what we have or haven't done, no matter what our shortcomings are. When we tap into the love—the kindness and compassion—that our true self has for the human that we are and for all of humanity, we unleash the power of love in our life to heal ourselves and others.

We desperately need this now on earth. Can you find it in your heart to be kind to yourself? This is not a selfish act, but the most unselfish act because it allows the love of your true nature to flow outward toward all of life. You don't have to like the ego and its ways; just accept it as part of the human condition. Be kind and compassionate toward yourself and those who are caught in the ego and the suffering it causes, and this kindness will release you and others from the ego's prison of limitation and fear. Love yourself and others for the courage to be alive and be human in these difficult and challenging times. Give yourself and others some slack. Forgive, allow, accept, and be kind. Relax and let everything be as it is.

57: HOPE AND FAITH

Hope is a positive belief about the future, while fear is a negative belief about the future. Both are beliefs and, as such, come from the ego. Hope is useful as an antidote to fear, which is a paralyzing and an unhappy state, and one we don't have to experience if we see the truth about fear—that it's an untrue belief about the future.

Hope can be useful in counteracting our fears and discouragement. However, once we are out of that negative state, hope can keep us from loving and accepting our life the way it is if we are hoping for something better or different than whatever is happening. Hoping that things will be different than they are may actually interfere with coping with or accepting not having what we want. Hope isn't always helpful even though it's better than fear.

Hope is a disguised desire. It's the belief that a desire will come true. Believing that is more pleasant and often more functional than believing the opposite. But the trouble with desires and beliefs is they keep us stuck in the ego. The result is that we bounce back and forth between hope and discouragement, between believing we'll get what we want and believing we won't.

This is where faith comes in. Faith is trusting that life is good, no matter what happens. Faith isn't a belief, although affirming that life is trustworthy can bring us into Essence, or the actual experience that life is trustworthy. When we are in Essence, we experience life as good, whatever is happening.

Hope and faith that life will turn out the way we (our ego) wants, on the other hand, is the ego's version of faith. That kind of faith is a belief and doesn't help us get what we want and may even interfere with that. It certainly doesn't help us be happy with the way things are. The ego is always living for a better future, and faith that we'll get what we want is just more of that.

The kind of faith that helps us be happy with the way things are is faith in the goodness of life, faith that whatever we are experiencing is the right experience, that it is serving life in some way. Who knows how it might be serving life? You may not know, but you trust that your experience is serving your soul and serving the Whole. That kind of faith helps you relax, let go, live in the moment, and experience your true nature. It helps you accept and make the best of the way things are for the time being. Accepting something doesn't mean not taking action to try to change what you'd like to change.

When you find within you that which is enjoying life just the way it is, then you have come Home, which is what we all really want. It's always possible to find this place of in-joy-ment and acceptance. Whenever we stop believing our thoughts, we experience it.

The way out of bouncing back and forth between thoughts of hope and thoughts of discouragement is to see that what you desire isn't always wise. Desires aren't always aligned with life's intentions, with what our soul, or Essence, intends for us. When our hopes and desires aren't aligned with Essence, we are bound to suffer. We see life as cruel, unfair, or random, and that just isn't so. Life has a plan for everyone, but that plan isn't always what we would like it to be. Life is wise and knows exactly how to evolve and shape us into an instrument for the Whole. When you aren't getting what you want, faith in life's goodness can help you accept and love your life the way it is. And that same faith will make it easier to make any constructive changes you are able to.

58: DEPTHS OF ESSENCE

Everyone experiences Essence. How could we not, when Essence is who we are? But Essence is covered over much of the time by identification with the false self, with the egoic mind. Just as clouds sometimes cover the sky, the false self covers over the true self. And like clouds, the false self can obscure the true self to varying degrees: On some days, there are only a few clouds, while on others, the sky is completely cloudy. Essence is experienced to varying degrees, depending on how involved we are with the egoic mind and how much of our attention is on the present moment.

Your attention might be bouncing back and forth between being present and being involved in thought. Or, it could be totally absorbed in thought. Or, if you have meditated or done other spiritual practices, you may have learned to be present much of the time. The longer we are able to be present, the deeper we go into Essence, which is why people often have the deepest experiences of Essence in meditation.

The point of meditation and any spiritual experiences that occur in or outside of meditation is to show us the truth and depth of our Being. Experiences of Oneness, Emptiness, or No Self show us the truth. And yet we have lives to live in this reality, so we return to ordinary consciousness, albeit altered by the experience. After seeing the truth, we don't view ourselves or anything else the same. Once the truth is known, it can't be forgotten.

Nevertheless, that depth of Essence can't be maintained amidst life. Functioning in the world requires a lesser experience of Essence. When we are present during our day, a subtle experience of Oneness is there, if we notice it. Life flows out of it. That attunement to Oneness calls forth certain responses and actions from us that are aligned with the Whole.

When we are learning to be more present in life, we move back and forth between being involved with the egoic mind and being present. If you are sufficiently present and not allowing your mind to interfere very much, you will enjoy what you are doing. When you find yourself enjoying even the simplest thing or something very ordinary or routine, you can be sure you are in Essence. When that happens, notice how you haven't been involved in thoughts about *me* and how it's going for *me*. Those are the thoughts that cause suffering. On the other hand, when you are barely present to what you are doing and absorbed in your thoughts, you won't be enjoying what you are doing. You will probably feel like you just want to get through it and on to something else. That's a sign you are more identified with the ego and your thoughts than with what's actually going on, with real life, with Essence.

It's possible to be using our functional mind and be very at peace. The egoic mind is the aspect of the mind that causes suffering, not the functional mind. When we do mental work, we become very focused and lose our sense of *me*, just as when we are meditating or absorbed in anything else. The problem with mental work, however, is that those who do a lot of it become very used to looking to the mind for answers and entertainment. A strong pathway to the mind is developed, and that pathway can just as easily take us to the egoic mind. So those who are intellectually inclined and do a lot of mental work may have more difficulty than others moving out of the egoic mind and staying in Essence. Meditation and physical activity are especially helpful in balancing any tendency to be overly mental.

We are happy, free, and at peace to the degree that we are in Essence and ignore the egoic mind. If you bounce back and forth between the egoic mind and Essence but live mostly in the egoic mind, you will still experience some happiness, freedom, and peace. On the other hand, if you are involved only a little with the egoic mind, you will experience much more peace and contentment. Or this could be said another way: If you are involved with the egoic mind most of the time, you will suffer a great deal; and if you are involved with it only a little, you will suffer only a little.

59: THE RIGHT DECISION

The ego is concerned about making the right decision. It sees things in black and white, good and bad, right and wrong. To the ego, if you don't make the *right* decision, you are making the *wrong* decision, and that's very bad for the ego's self-image. The ego is always trying to get things right and avoid being wrong, according to its beliefs, desires, and values—and other people's too. Doing this, the ego presumes, will ensure it is on top and that it will survive this dog-eat-dog world. The ego's worldview comes from feeling separate from others and life. The sense of being separate is, in fact, the definition of the ego.

The ego maintains this sense of separateness and individuality in part through judgment: "This is good and what I want, and that's bad and what I don't want. This is me, and that's not me." Everything is put into boxes: "what I like and what I don't like, what I want and what I don't want, what I believe and what I don't believe, those who are like me and those who aren't like me." The ego creates adversaries and friends this way. It creates enmity and conflict by viewing life this way.

The ego's view of life is false. Things and people can't be put into boxes so easily. Life is full of complexities, and everyone and everything is unique. The ego can't deal with life's complexity, so it categorizes people and everything else. Of course, language is very much a part of this process, and why the ego's way of thinking is so deeply embedded in us. Language creates concepts, and concepts get in the way of experiencing life purely and moving through life more naturally and simply. "Right" is a concept, as is "wrong." In truth, there is no right decision. Whatever is deemed right is deemed right by only one thing—the ego.

Who we really are, Essence, doesn't experience life conceptually, but simply and purely. It just experiences. Decisions aren't made, but come out of the flow of life naturally. Making a decision is definitely an act of the ego. It makes a decision happen. Sometimes that decision is in the flow, and sometimes it isn't. Whatever decision is made is accepted by Essence and worked with, although Essence might still try to steer us in another direction.

Essence co-creates life with the ego. Essence plays it by ear and expresses itself through us as much as we allow it to. Essence also allows us to express the ego, since all choices eventually take us Home. Along the way, there is plenty to experience, enjoy, and grow from, no matter what is chosen. Some paths will be easier, some will be more intense, some will be slower, and some will be faster, but they all bring wisdom and they all teach love.

From the ego's point of view, a good decision is one that reaps desirable results, and a bad one reaps the opposite. Essence, on the other hand, often welcomes and even creates difficult or challenging situations because it values the growth, learning, and character that can come from them. Essence doesn't just accept challenges, it builds them into life, it designs them, it loves them.

Whether we are aligned with Essence or not, we will experience challenges. They can't be avoided. What's important is how we deal with them. Will you let them make you stronger? Will you learn from them? Will you become more compassionate, or bitter or disheartened? Will you open your heart instead of closing it? How we respond to difficulties and challenges determines whether life feels good and meaningful or not, not the absence of difficulties.

The ego believes the absence of difficulties is the goal and the ideal, which is impossible. Not a soul on earth has ever had a life like that, and never will. Life just isn't designed that way. The ego's ideas about life don't match the reality, so it's no wonder the ego is always unhappy and complaining. When we expect something to be other than the way it is, we suffer. And the ego expects life to be the way it wants to be, as if its desires determine all that is right and good in the world.

It's good to recognize the ego's lies because then they lose their power to undermine our happiness. This is freedom—seeing the truth. And then nothing else has to change. The way to a happy life is not in making the *right* decision, but in being aligned with the truth about life. When we are, deciding just comes out of the flow, and it feels just right.

60: SUCCESS

So many people are driven by the desire for success. What is success? If success is a desire of yours, what does it mean to you? How will you know when you achieve it? What will it look and feel like? Such questions help us discover what our idea of success is. Success is an idea.

We imagine success will look and feel a certain way—and won't that be wonderful! Everyone wants life to be wonderful—always, unendingly. And yet no one in the world has ever achieved that. Life is sometimes wonderful, according to the ego, but it's also not so wonderful, according to the ego. As long as the ego is involved, its fantasies will be the only thing about life that will be consistently wonderful, which is why the ego loves its fantasies so much.

Like all fantasies, the fantasy of success has all advantages and no disadvantages. Have you ever noticed how your fantasies don't include the negatives? That's why they are so appealing. When you dream of success, you don't imagine you'll have to hire and manage a staff, deal with hundreds of emails and phone calls a day, and meet with as much controversy as praise. Fantasies leave a lot out.

Think of the times you have dreamed of something—a relationship, a car, a home—and then you got it, only to discover that it wasn't the perfectly wonderful experience you dreamed of. It needed maintenance and care, effort and attention. That's real life. What the ego often does as a result of that reality is seek a different relationship (or none), a different car, or a different home. A lot of change happens because of the ego's never-ending search to once and for all feel good and be happy. The solution can't be found in what created the problem (the ego), but only in what is beyond the ego.

What do you really want from being successful? Admiration? Security? Peace? Freedom? Love? A beautiful home? These are things the ego wants. Success is a machination of the ego. It isn't real. The proof is that no two people have the same definition of success. It's a concept. It doesn't represent anything real. Therefore, it can't ever be attained. It's like a mirage that is forever just out of reach. From the standpoint of your youth, you are probably successful now in many ways. You probably have more knowledge, wisdom, experience, abilities, and perhaps even more money and material things. But you still might not define yourself as successful. Why not? Because our criteria for success keep changing: As soon as we become successful, our definition of success changes.

What if you realized that you are already successful? What would that be like? How would that feel? The truth is we are totally successful at having the experiences we are having. We are totally successful at being. We have never been anything but successful from the standpoint of Essence.

Why not take the standpoint of Essence? It really is your choice. You can choose to see yourself as successful right now. What a relief! No more struggle required. You can just rest. Isn't that all you have ever really wanted anyhow? Peace and contentment are yours by just seeing the truth: You have already "made it" when you see that peace and happiness are already here. You have already "arrived" when you discover there was never anywhere to go.

61: SADNESS AND GRIEF

Sadness may seem like an inevitable part of life, but sadness can't be perpetuated without a sad story. It's not that sadness shouldn't happen in response to an event, but it can't be maintained without remembering a sad event or telling a story about that event. And a lot of sadness doesn't stem from any event, but from a perception or belief, such as: "I will never be happy." "I will always be a failure." "I am ugly." "No one will ever love me." "Life is cruel."

Sadness is a natural response to loss. There's nothing wrong with sadness or grief. However, there's much more sadness in the world than there needs to be. So much unnecessary sadness is generated by how we think about things and by remembering unfortunate events. The natural grieving process is extended through memory and by repeating a sad story related to that memory. It goes something like this: "It should never have happened. I will never be happy again. This is so terrible. I can't bear it." Sadness is evoked whenever those thoughts are believed or repeated to others. A good question is, "What am I telling myself that makes me feel sad?"

It doesn't take much to create sadness, just a memory or the repetition of a sad story. Even someone else's sad story can make us sad. People love sad stories. It gets them in touch with their compassion for others, which feels good. But telling our own sad story and crying over it isn't an experience of compassion as much as victimization. The ego actually enjoys feeling like a victim to some extent because that gives it an identity: "I'm a victim." An identity keeps the illusion of I (the false self) going and keeps us engaged with the ego instead of being present to what's going on right now. When we are feeling a lot of sadness, the ego will pose a solution or plan of action that further involves us with our thoughts and feelings.

Sadness is an emotion that appears to be a problem to solve. Unpleasant emotions are uncomfortable and beg to be resolved. The ego creates problems (feelings), and then it tries to solve them, which is how the ego keeps us identified with it. If you buy into the ego's perceptions and the feelings and problems created by those perceptions, you are likely to buy into its solutions. Since other people are often more than happy to agree with our sad stories and the ego's solutions, because they have egos themselves that tell similar stories, others often aren't that helpful in getting us beyond our sad stories.

Is it true that something shouldn't have happened? It may be true that you didn't want something to happen, but it's not true that it shouldn't have happened. Who says so? The ego. But that declaration doesn't make it so. Life is the way it is. Things happen the way they happen, and who knows why? Death, loss, and hardship happen. They are part of life. To say that they shouldn't happen is to disagree with the way things are, and when we do that, we suffer. The ego is angry when things don't go its way. It feels like life is out to get it, but that isn't true. Life just is the way it is. The hardships and losses we experience aren't personal. The proof is that hardships and losses happen to everyone. No one escapes challenges.

Since we don't have control over what happens and since loss and other unfortunate things do happen, the only recourse is to accept them and not take them personally. To do anything other than that is to create suffering for ourselves. Telling ourselves a sad (and untrue) story creates unnecessary suffering. The unfortunate event is over, and it can only live on by remembering it, by thinking about it. Does it serve a purpose to keep it alive through memory? That's a very good question. What purpose does doing that serve? What do you get out of doing that? Or what are you trying to accomplish by doing that?

Some people feel they are being disloyal to a lost loved one if they don't bring that person up in memory and perpetuate the grieving process. But it doesn't serve us or those who are gone to do that. Not only do we create unnecessary sadness for ourselves, but our grief may also delay our loved one's adjustment to his or her new life in another dimension. Letting go of the past doesn't mean letting go of our love for someone. Love can never be lost. But when the person we love is no longer in our life, that must be accepted so that we can be present to the life that is being born out of the present moment.

Life keeps being birthed. It continues to bring new things, people, events, love, and opportunities to us. If we are lost in grief, we may miss the beauty of what life is offering us now. Sadness doesn't just make us sad, it takes us out of the present, where true happiness and the movement of life is happening. Sadness serves no one but the ego.

62: WHAT YOU DON'T HAVE TO ACCEPT

Acceptance is an important spiritual teaching because the ego is so unaccepting of the way life is. Therefore, acceptance can move us out of the ego and into Essence, which accepts whatever is going on. Acceptance is a spiritual tool that counteracts, or neutralizes, the ego and drops us into Essence. Acceptance, however, doesn't mean doing nothing about whatever is going on; it means accepting whatever is going on, and then responding to that from Essence. Not accepting what's going on keeps us identified with the ego and its responses to what's going on. That's why acceptance is important—because it drops us into Essence, which knows how to respond kindly, compassionately, and wisely to any situation. If you don't want the ego to be the one responding to whatever is going on, then first accept what's going on, and then see how Essence moves you in the moment.

People often assume that accepting a situation means not attempting to change it or not removing yourself from it. That's a key misunderstanding. For instance, if someone is acting unkindly or abusively, you accept that that is happening (because it is!), and then you respond from Essence. That response is likely to be a rational one, not an emotional one, since the ego is what creates emotions. Essence might express compassion or say something to bring calm and peace to the situation. Or Essence might remove you from the situation without saying a word. Or perhaps there's something to be learned from the situation that will register within you intuitively, which you'll be able to catch if you aren't caught up in the ego's negative emotions. Essence doesn't accept abuse or unkindness. It accepts that it's happening, but Essence doesn't allow it to continue, although Essence doesn't respond abusively or unkindly to it. This is an important distinction.

When we are identified with the ego, we react automatically to unkindness and abuse in primarily two ways, both of which are dysfunctional: We get angry, judge, criticize, or in some other way try to hurt the abusive person. Or, if unworthiness or being a victim is part of our self-image, we allow the abuse to continue, blame ourselves for it, and feel sad and worthless. If people in our childhood were unkind to us, then we are likely to accept unkind treatment from others because that's what we expect and are used to or what we think we deserve.

If criticism, blame, anger, judgment, and abuse are the primary ways someone is interacting with you, then acceptance means accepting that that's happening and also accepting that you don't like it and aren't willing to allow yourself to be abused and then giving yourself the gift of getting out of that environment. Essence is wise enough to choose a more loving environment, even if it means being alone. Essence accepts that egos can be mean and nasty, but it does whatever is necessary to create an inner and outer environment in which peace and love can thrive. Essence moves, always, in the direction of love, and that means loving ourselves enough to not accept unkindness and abuse.

By the way, not accepting negative behavior is also in the abusive person's highest good because that person needs to understand the impact of such behavior and not have it reinforced by us. This is why we send children to their room when they misbehave, isn't it? In doing this, we are saying, "I love you and accept you, but this behavior is unacceptable." We distance ourselves from a child who behaves badly by isolating them, and this accomplishes two things: The behavior isn't reinforced and we say no to participating in a negative environment and yes to creating a more loving one.

63: THE BLAME GAME

It probably comes as no surprise to anyone that blaming is entirely the ego's thing and never comes from a place of alignment with Essence. Still, even when we know this, we may fall prey to blaming because we are wired, or programmed, to blame others. Blaming is an automatic and therefore often unconscious response. The thing about unconscious responses is that we don't question them. And the thing about our programming is that we believe it, that is, we really believe someone or something else is to blame when that's what we are thinking and feeling. Our thoughts and feelings are so convincing that even when we can see how useless and even destructive blame is, we still do it.

Our only recourse is to become more conscious of thoughts of blame when they arise, to recognize them as the ego's defense mechanism and a way of coping with difficulties, and then to choose not to indulge those thoughts, which can quickly turn into feelings that compel us to act in angry and punishing ways. It's essential to catch the idea that someone or something is to blame *before* that thought becomes strengthened by feelings.

Watch the mind as it tries to pin blame on one thing or another. It scrambles from one opinion or theory to another, or it comes to a conclusion immediately. When something happens that we don't like, this blame machinery instantly kicks in. "What or who is to blame?" is often one of the first thoughts that comes to mind. The trouble with this question is that there is no simple answer, although the ego doesn't acknowledge the complexity of life.

The ego operates very much from a framework of cause and effect: One cause creates one effect. But life isn't like that. For example, we think that if someone harms someone or something, then the person who performed that action is the cause of the harm. But what led up to that person doing that? There are many causes for that behavior, not only that person's past experiences and personal conditioning, but that person's cultural conditioning, including the media and the times we live in. There are genetic, physical, mental, environmental, personality-based, history-based, human, cultural, karmic, and other influences and contributors to every action. When it comes to our choices, it may seem like we have free will, but the combination of our conditioning and other influences often compels us to make choices that aren't really very free. This is not to excuse harmful behavior, but to point out that placing blame is not that easy.

Moreover, blaming others is a dysfunctional response, meaning it doesn't change what happened and it doesn't improve or fix the situation. In fact, blame keeps us in the grip of the ego, where we are out of touch with the wisdom, acceptance, compassion, and truer perspective of Essence, which responds to life wisely, rationally, and in a way that heals and helps the situation. To the ego, bringing acceptance to a situation we don't like seems ludicrous, and yet, it is acceptance that allows us to access the wisdom, peace, and equanimity of our true self and act from that place instead of from the ego's narrow, destructive perspective.

Blaming is one of the easiest things in the world to do because following the ego's programming is what is easiest for us to do. Unfortunately, blaming leads to more unhappiness and pain. It doesn't make sense that what is automatic and feels true to do is actually the destructive thing to do, but then again, when we are in the grip of the ego, we don't care if we are being destructive.

However, blame is not only destructive to others, but also to ourselves. And that's what must be seen. It isn't hard to see this if we are willing to notice the effect that blame has on our bodies and consciousness. Blame causes us to contract and feel terrible. If it weren't for the sense it gives us of being right, we probably wouldn't indulge in it as much as we do. But blame gives us a sense of being right as well as a false sense that we are doing something about the problem, when actually we aren't bringing anything constructive to the situation.

Trying to come up with answers to who or what is to blame for something is a fruitless exercise. It's a waste of our time and energy. Worst of all, it removes us from the place where love and wisdom flow, and that's a terrible punishment to heap upon ourselves. The beauty and power of forgiveness is that it takes us out of blame. It redeems us from the grasp of the ego and drops us back into Essence, where we belong.

64: TWO KINDS OF HAPPINESS

True happiness comes from reality, from what is present in our environment and from what is coming in through our senses, and this happiness can be experienced anytime. There's another kind of happiness that is unreal and doesn't last, and that's the happiness that comes from getting what we want. The ego has ideas about what it wants and needs to be happy, and when life provides that, an emotion that we identify as happiness is experienced. This emotion comes from the ego and, like every other emotion, comes and goes relatively quickly. This emotion of happiness, unlike the other emotions produced by the ego, is a pleasant one, although it's not so pleasant when it disappears.

This emotion of happiness is also often the result of giving meaning to an event. For instance, you feel happy and excited when you're making more money, not just because you want more money, but because you think having money means something: "I'm finally succeeding," "People like me," "I'm worthwhile." Getting what we want often results in the ego telling a good story, and we feel happy—until something we don't like happens, and the story turns bad.

The ego's happiness is often experienced as a high, and we get addicted, in a sense, to feeling this emotional high. We want to feel it all the time, although that's impossible. We seek it and try to get it to last, but the seeking and trying to maintain this kind of happiness is actually a place of suffering. Like all emotions, the happiness of the ego dissipates and is replaced by the more usual egoic state of disappointment and striving. The ego continues to go after whatever gives it this high, not realizing that there's another kind of happiness that doesn't come and go. That happiness is real, or true, happiness.

True happiness occurs when we are in contact with real life and with what is experiencing real life—our true self, or Essence. Thoughts are part of real life, but they create a virtual reality that takes us out of real life and into a mental world. This mental world can't deliver the kind of happiness that is possible from the real world, although thinking is enjoyable to some extent, which is what makes thoughts enticing. If thoughts weren't sometimes pleasurable, they would be much easier to ignore. The trouble with thoughts is that they replace real experience, which is even more enjoyable than thinking. And of course, the problem with thoughts is that many thoughts produced by the ego take us down a path of worry, fear, struggle, and striving.

The real world is inherently pleasurable because experiencing it is essentially an experience of what is coming in through our senses, and that's generally pleasurable. Even unpleasant sensory experiences are interesting and can be entertaining. For example, rock concerts are still stimulating and interesting even though the music is loud, chaotic, and not generally considered pleasant. Essence is very interested in having all types of sensory experiences. Every experience is something new and unique. We enjoy new experiences not only for the possible pleasure they might bring, but simply because they are new and different.

When we are present to real life, however it is showing up, happiness is possible because Essence is fascinated by the experience it is having and wondering what will happen next. It relishes even the little things that show up in each moment. Everything we experience when we are aligned with our true self feels like such a miracle. The sense of awe and wonder of being present to real life as it's showing up is true happiness. It doesn't get any better than that. And the happiness of our true self is always available, since real life is always right here, right now to be experienced.

The only thing that interferes with this simple experience of awe and wonder is the egoic mind, which discounts and is disappointed in real life. But that is the ego's story, and that's the lie that is behind all suffering. There is nothing disappointing or lacking in real life. It is a great miracle, and Essence is loving it all. This love for life is true happiness.

65: COMPARISONS

The ego is always making comparisons. It sizes people and situations up: "Am I better or worse than that person?" "Is this situation better or worse for me?" The ego also compares the present with an ideal image, a fantasy, which leaves the present coming up short. Making such comparisons wouldn't be so bad if it served a purpose, but all it does is make us discontent. Even when we come out superior, it doesn't feel good or satisfy us, but makes us feel petty and mean. Everyone would live much better without making comparisons, which only take us out of the present moment, where we can act most effectively.

Comparisons take us out of the real world, out of the moment, and involve us in a world of concepts. "Better" is a concept; there is no such thing. The mind decides what is better according to its ideas. "Better" is one more idea the ego generates about its own ideas. "Better" is often integral to the stories it tells: "Other people are better educated than me, so I'll never succeed." "She is prettier than me, so she gets all the men." "I'm not as good as everyone else, so I'll never be happy."

The problem isn't so much in acknowledging that something or someone is better in some way, but in the meaning given to that. It may be a fact that someone is, for instance, a better tennis player than someone else. That's no problem—everyone's different. But when we assume that that means something else, we have just moved into the ego's realm of make-believe. The ego makes up stories about what being better or worse mean and then suffers over them.

Comparisons keep us in a world of dissatisfaction because the ego tends to draw comparisons that make us feel unhappy and dissatisfied. They leave us feeling like we aren't enough or don't have enough. They cause us to notice what we don't have, not what we do have. The ego is behind the "glass is half empty" syndrome. It doesn't notice what's here, only what isn't. Only when we compare what we have with someone who has far less, do we appreciate what we do have. The ego doesn't draw these types of comparisons, however, because it's in the business of creating discontentment.

To counteract the ego's tendency to notice what it doesn't have, it can be helpful to establish a habit of noticing what you do have, of counting your blessings. Gratitude, which is a quality of Essence, is the antidote to the ego's comparisons. We cultivate gratitude by noticing what we are grateful for instead of focusing on what's missing or what we desire, as the ego does.

Expressing gratitude drops us into Essence because gratitude is the experience of our true self. Essence is exceedingly grateful just to experience this life, and it's grateful for every aspect of creation and every kind of experience. We feel this too when we are in Essence. When that happens, notice the gratitude, and in noticing it, the gratitude becomes magnified. By doing the opposite of what the ego does, you will find yourself in love with life, just as Essence is. And you will discover there is already plenty here for your happiness and more peace than you ever expected.

66: TRUSTING YOUR HEART

We all know what it means to follow our Heart. We know because the Heart is an experience everyone has, as difficult as it is to describe. People want to follow their Heart, but they don't always know what their Heart is telling them or trust it.

What is so hard about trusting the Heart, when the Heart actually has a very good reputation? You don't hear people saying, "Be careful—don't trust your Heart too much!" Rather, they tell you to trust your Heart. What keeps us from doing that then? The answer is: thoughts of doubt and worry that stir up fear. Fear makes our doubts and worries seem true. The ego tricks us into believing these thoughts instead of our Heart by producing fear, tension, and contraction in our body, which make these thoughts seem true and necessary to our survival. Pretty tricky, isn't it?

Wisdom resides in the Heart, not in the mind. The functional mind is helpful, but wisdom is required in applying the mind's information to specific situations. Have you noticed that wisdom doesn't come from the mind, although it might be mulled over in the mind? Wisdom is more of a knowing than a thought.

There's a big difference between a knowing and a thought. A knowing is felt in the body, often like a download of information. A knowing is nonlinear and not experienced as words until we think about it and put it into words. Thoughts, on the other hand, appear as words in our mind. There is no knowing before the words appear. The words appear seemingly out of nowhere. They actually come from the unconscious, which is the storehouse of conditioning.

The problem with most thoughts is that they are conditioning that is part of the false self, which isn't wise. Conditioning is only so useful. It includes stored beliefs, attitudes, perspectives, opinions, teachings, and judgments, many of which are contradictory or untrue. Even conditioning that is generally true may not be true for a given situation, so this storehouse of information and beliefs is not that useful for guiding our life. It's information about what you have done in the past and what others have done, but that information is only so helpful for the present moment.

Wisdom, unlike thoughts, comes to us intuitively, not mentally. Intuitions don't arrive in our mind, but in our body. Some people feel them in the center of their body, in the solar plexus or slightly higher, in what is known as the Heart center. Wisdom comes from Essence, which communicates regularly this way. Intuition is the means by which Essence communicates with the character we are playing in this lifetime. The egoic mind, on the other hand, is the means by which the ego communicates with this character and upholds the identity of this character.

Occasionally, Essence uses the mind to communicate. When it does, Essence's communications feel very different from the ego's, which generally cause us to contract and feel confused, tense, dissatisfied, or any number of other negative feelings. When Essence uses the mind to communicate, words pop into our mind and feel surprising, right, refreshing, expansive, inspiring, and uplifting. They ring true immediately. Essence's communications are very brief and don't go on and on like the mind's. They are pithy and to the point, and then they are gone. Everyone has had many experiences of these types of communications. You know them when you experience them. That is the Heart's wisdom, and it can be trusted.

It's possible for Essence's wisdom to be what guides you in your life all the time. All it takes is a willingness to notice and respond to your intuition instead of trying to figure out answers with the mind first. The ego is impatient and wants answers to life's questions now, so the ego makes up answers. The ego's guidance about what to do are based on "shoulds" and other conditioning. If you listen to your thoughts instead of waiting for the true answer to show up intuitively, the ego may take you down a different path than Essence would. Following the Heart often requires some patience and always requires trusting our innate wisdom rather than our thoughts.

67: HONESTY

If honesty were always the best policy, there wouldn't be a debate about it or even the need for such an aphorism. We would just practice honesty. The truth is (pardon the pun) that honesty is not always the best policy if honesty comes from the ego. You could say that there are two kinds of truths: the ego's truth and Essence's. When people encourage us to speak our truth, they are referring to Essence's truth, not the ego's.

The ego's truth is more like an untruth because it is based on conditioned beliefs, preferences, desires, and feelings. For instance, when you tell someone that he or she is messy, that isn't *the* truth, it isn't even *your* truth (your true self's truth), but your false self's truth, and that just isn't very true. Our conditioning isn't any truer than someone else's, even though the ego believes it is.

Speaking the false self's truth has no value. The proof is in the fruits, in the results. Does what you are saying bring you closer to love and unity with others? If it doesn't, then what you are saying isn't essentially true. It's a small truth, the ego's truth, based on its conditioning. What is essentially true (true from Essence's standpoint) will bear positive fruits and result in love, not contraction, fear, or conflict, which are not desirable fruits. The ego's words bear negative fruits, while Essence's bear love and peace.

There's no honor in honesty for honesty's sake when that honesty comes from the ego. Honesty is not honorable when it results in contraction, conflict, or hurt. Honesty sometimes pretends to be honorable when it isn't. The ego often uses it as a weapon. The underlying intent of being honest may be to try to change or manipulate others, not help or support them. Honesty can be a disguised judgment.

It's easy to tell when the ego is talking. When you give voice to the ego, it doesn't feel good. You feel contracted and self-righteous. You can also tell if your words are coming from the ego by how they make others feel. Although we aren't responsible for other people's feelings, and sometimes truth that comes from Essence isn't what someone wants to hear, the ego's words tend to be *intentionally* hurtful because they are often an attempt to be right or superior.

Words from Essence, on the other hand, feel good as they are being spoken and as they are being received, or at least true. The atmosphere relaxes, softens, and people feel loved, expansive, and good, or at least receptive to what is being said. There's always something kind and loving that Essence could say that is true. When we drop into Essence, we see things differently, more positively, more graciously. We notice what we love about life, others, and ourselves. We may say very different things than our ego would say, but they'll be true. They won't just be "white lies" to be nice. They'll come from the place within us that delights in people's differences and even in their personal quirks.

Essence sees the same things the ego sees, but Essence loves it all. What a difference it makes to speak the truth and have that feel good and ignite love instead of conflict. It's always possible to speak the truth and be loving. So be sure to speak your truth, but make it Essence's truth rather than the ego's, and your life will be transformed.

68: CHIPPING AWAY AT CONDITIONING

You can become free of your conditioning running you. You have probably already experienced some conditioning disappearing, since a natural healing process is occurring in everyone as part of our spiritual evolution. Becoming free of our conditioning can be a slow process, however, so slow that it may seem like nothing is happening. The process is similar to chopping down a tree: You chip, chip, chip away at it, and it doesn't budge, until finally one last stroke of the ax brings the tree down. Bringing down conditioning often requires being aware of it without identifying with it many, many times—possibly hundreds, even thousands, of times—before those thoughts no longer arise. One day, it dawns on you that things are different: You aren't bothered with those thoughts anymore. What a miracle!

Whenever we identify with a certain thought, that thought is strengthened, or reinforced. It might be something like: "I'll never by happy." "I'm stupid." "People don't like me." "I have to be perfect." If a thought has strong feelings attached to it, it has probably been reinforced by identifying with it and believing it repeatedly. The strength of a thought isn't proof that it is true, but signifies that it's been reinforced and believed many times. For this reason, core beliefs can be hard to overcome, but not impossible. Any negative thoughts that arise frequently and strongly in our mind need to be seen for what they are: untrue and unhelpful.

The way to chip away at negative conditioning is to, first, become aware of your negative thoughts. Then recognize that they are just conditioning and not true. Seeing the truth about your negative thoughts—that they aren't true or valuable—allows you to get some distance from them and not automatically identify with them. The habit is to be unconscious of thoughts and react to them emotionally and in other ways, which only reinforces them.

To turn this habit around, you have to become aware of the thoughts that make you feel bad. Once you have become aware of these thoughts, it's possible to see that they belong to a negative voice within you, the ego, that has no truth. Before that, this voice seemed like it was telling you something true about yourself. Once you realize that that voice is a lie and doesn't serve you, those thoughts will stop affecting you. If you don't believe them, it doesn't matter if they continue to show up. If you consistently disidentify with those thoughts, they will eventually stop arising, although they may have to be seen for what they are many times before that happens.

The thoughts that show up repeatedly in our mind that create contraction or negative feelings are the ones that are meant to be healed. They are the ones we are conscious of, so they are the ones that are ready to be healed. As we clear away one piece of conditioning, another will take its place in line to be healed. That is how the unconscious is cleared.

The good news is that to be free, it isn't necessary to clear away every piece of conditioning. At a certain point, you really get that all of the thoughts in the egoic mind are false or unnecessary, and you just don't get involved in any of them anymore. Freedom doesn't require healing or abolishing all conditioning, only fully recognizing it for what it is. However, some conditioning, especially thoughts that evoke strong emotions, may require some inquiry and healing work to weed out the complex of misunderstandings and untruths that hold that conditioning in place.

69: WHAT ABOUT THE PERSONALITY?

Most of you reading this are pretty clear that you aren't your personality. Spiritual experiences bring us the realization that we aren't just physical beings, but spiritual beings in a physical body. The human vehicle that Consciousness is inhabiting includes a mind, conditioning, an ego, and a personality. This human vehicle is programmed to behave and respond to life in a certain way.

Part of this programming is the ego, which every human being has. The ego gives us the sense that we are an individual. Without this, we wouldn't answer when someone called our name or be able to function. So the ego serves the Creator, the Oneness, by creating the illusion that we are separate individuals rather than all One, as we are in truth. In addition to causing a sense of being separate from other human beings, the ego causes us to have certain desires—the desire for money, power, security, safety, recognition, comfort, superiority, and so on. These desires actually stem from the sense of separateness, and they result in the various human emotions: anger, hatred, greed, lust, jealousy, pride, shame, guilt, fear, hopelessness, depression, resentment, envy, and sadness.

Each of us also has other desires and drives that are unique to us, which also are part of our programming. These desires and drives are reflected in the personality, and they can be read in the astrology chart. For instance, Aries represents a drive to pioneer, lead, initiate activity, and try new things, and these drives are reflected in a personality that is courageous, individualistic, bold, and independent. The programming represented in the astrology chart determines, to a large extent, the personality, which is different from the ego.

The personality is the costume we wear. This costume is unlike anyone else's costume, and we don't lose it (our personality) after we awaken and realize our true nature. The ego, on the other hand, is what prevents us from experiencing our true nature. As we evolve spiritually, the ego falls into the background and Essence expresses itself through our personality more. When that happens, our personality becomes more loving and likeable. Our costume becomes colored by the love, peace, contentment, and wisdom of Essence. On the other hand, when the ego expresses itself through our costume, it (our personality) is colored by the self-interest, drives, fears, and other emotions of the ego.

The experience of our true nature is an experience of emptiness, of no qualities, no gender, nothingness. The Nothingness needs a costume to be seen, heard, and felt! How can Nothingness be seen and express itself in the world without a costume? It needs some clothes, so it takes on programming (a personality, as represented in the astrology chart) to give it some clothes. And since it makes no sense for the Nothingness to look the same and have the same expression in every human being, each person is given unique programming/clothing. What fun it is for the Nothingness to play with itself in all these different forms! It really doesn't know how this is all going to go—how all these expressions of itself will play and what they will do together. That's really fun too.

70: SILENCE IS GOLDEN

"Silence is golden" acknowledges the spiritual reality that is uncovered and discovered in silence. The silence that is golden is not the absence of sound, for sound can actually bring us into Essence, but the absence of mental noise, which often spills out through people's mouths as chatter. In those rare moments when the mind is quiet, the golden radiance of Essence can be experienced subtly. The world looks and feels different when the mental chatter has ceased and the silent stillness of our true nature is experienced. Then experiencing life purely without the filter of the mind is possible. When that happens, life takes on a beautiful and peaceful subtle radiance.

The absence of egoic thought allows for the quiet Presence that we are to be experienced. Thoughts are noisy, whether they are inside our head or expressed. Thoughts attract and demand our attention, pulling it away from what's real and true about life. Thoughts are manufactured by the ego and reflect its values. They demand this and that from life, complain, fuss, and fume. All this negativity is hard to ignore. Our thoughts give us the impression that there's a problem we need to do something about. Like a screaming child, the egoic mind is difficult to ignore and silence. It seems that attending to it is the way to silence it, but the opposite is true. Getting involved with those thoughts only keeps the noise going.

When we are identified with our thoughts, we are agitated, contracted, and ill at ease. But once you realize that there is a silent Watcher who is disengaged from them and resting in silence apart from them, you can begin to tap into the potential of your true nature for peace. You are this Watcher, not the chattering mind. You have a mind, but you are not the mind. You are the space in which thoughts appear. That space is silent, all-encompassing, embracing, and allowing. It receives and allows everything that is happening without being touched by it. You are that silent, yet deeply rich and infinite, space. The space becomes filled with chatter at times, but the space remains the same: pure, unblemished, and unchanged.

When you put your attention on that space or on the silence in between your thoughts, you fall into the spaciousness of your Being. You become it, if even for just a brief second. The more you notice that space, the more familiar with it you become, and the more you are able to see the truth about it—that it is who you are. That silent, all-accepting, conscious space is what everyone and everything else emanate from. Consciousness is what you are.

You are not the petty voice of the ego. Our true self is hidden from us by the false one. Waking up to the truth only requires accepting the possibility that you are far grander than you have ever imagined. You are not any of your self-images, but beyond all images and all thoughts. You are the space in which thought emerges and the space in between the thoughts. The silence in between thoughts is golden because, like gold, it is precious, pure, eternal, and true, unlike thoughts. By simply putting your attention on silence, you become it: Everything stills, and there you are!

71: THE RIGHT EXPERIENCE

The ego is always looking for a better experience—the right experience. The truth is that you are having the right experience and always have been! What if you really knew that? Just take this in for a moment: The experience you are having right now is the right experience. It's the experience you *should* be having. Despite how the ego feels, the present moment shouldn't be different! It has been co-created by you, by the Oneness, and by everything else that exists in creation. It's a miraculous dance between you, the Oneness, and everything that has brought you to the present moment.

We are part of a greater Whole, and we move within that Whole. We move in response to everything in the Whole, and everything else does too. We aren't responsible for what is arising in the moment except for our interpretation of it. That is where our power lies. We have the power to interpret our reality and thereby determine our experience of it. We are programmed with certain interpretations, certain beliefs and other ideas about life. We automatically accept them because they are our programming. However, at any point, we can change those interpretations to ones that are wiser, truer, and more loving than the faulty programming we have been given.

For many, it's time for the programming to be overwritten or erased and for the truth to take its place. The old programming was false. The new program is simple: You are Consciousness living through a body-mind and experiencing life and fulfilling a particular plan that serves the Whole. You don't know the plan ahead of time, but it's revealed to you in each moment, as you respond purely to what is arising in the Now. This may seem unbelievable and impossible, but more and more people are waking up out of the old programming and beginning to live just this way.

There is an Intelligence behind all life. You are that Intelligence as it manifests through your particular body-mind. It's moving and awakening each of us from the egoic nightmare at exactly the right time. When people hear about awakening, it often becomes one more thing to desire and attain and suffer over. But awakening isn't something you have to strive for. You are waking up to your ability to choose the ego or Essence, and the degree to which you are doing that is exactly right for now.

Where you are in your evolution is exactly where you are meant to be. How could it be otherwise? The ego is the only thing that sees where you are at as not good enough. It simply isn't true that you or your consciousness should be anywhere other than where you or it is right now. Each of our lives is unfolding as it needs to as part of this dance of the Whole. It can't be any different than the way it is right now. And like every dance, timing is everything! The Intelligence that we are knows exactly how to unfold our plans and wake us up, so we can just relax and enjoy the great mystery that we are part of. You are having exactly the right experience.

Notice how you can relax when you believe this. And from that relaxation and peace, much good can come because you aren't busy striving for something else. From that peace, it's easy to respond to life naturally, from the essential goodness that you are. However, it was never a mistake to strive, any more than it's a mistake to stop striving. When you were striving, that was the right experience, and when you stop striving, that is the right experience. The Whole determines when that will be, more than our individual will.

We are so much greater than we *think* we are. We are more like a cell in the body of this Intelligence, and like a cell, each of us has a part to play that is necessary to the Whole. You are already playing that part and always have been. You can't help but play that part, but that part will be more enjoyable if you realize that you are already fulfilling your role within the Whole.

72: THE TYRANNY OF TIME

Time is a concept, so it's impossible to have too much or too little. No matter how busy we are, it is never true that we don't have enough time. How can you not have enough of something that doesn't exist? Time is a useful concept, especially for arranging meetings, but it's become a tyrant in many people's minds.

The ego creates the sense of not having enough time by arbitrarily deciding what must get done in a day. The ego could just as easily decide to get less done, but it doesn't do that because it is in the business of pushing us to achieve its goals, become better (according to its definition), and get more of everything. It pushes us to do these things because it thinks they will lead to happiness and security.

The ego uses time to push us by assigning lots to do in a day and then monitoring how well we are accomplishing those things. The ego tells us what to get done and evaluates how well we are doing it. It's like having a tyrant or boss in our head. The tyrant is externalized in bosses and other authority figures, who act out this part of us and cause us stress, just as the internal tyrant does.

Notice how often you feel like you don't have enough time and how that affects you. What's that like? Believing you don't have enough time makes you feel tense and contracted because it isn't true that you don't have enough time. Untrue thoughts make us feel tense and contracted.

"Not enough time" is the ego's negative spin on life. There's never enough of anything for the ego, so naturally there isn't enough time either, even when there is. Have you ever noticed how the tyranny around time continues even when you aren't busy? On the weekend, for instance, you might feel like you don't have enough time to relax or do what you'd like to do. The egoic mind imagines it needs more time to be happy, and that idea causes unhappiness! Having too much work or not enough play both feel like not having enough time. Time is just one more way the ego inserts its point of view of "not enough" into the moment.

When we feel like we don't have enough time, we rush around, act frustrated, and feel stressed. But what creates the feeling of being stressed is the *idea* that we don't have enough time or ideas about what we are doing rather than what we are actually doing. We can just as easily be very busy and not feel stressed and rushed. We all have had the experience many times of enjoying having a lot to do.

The idea that we don't have enough time is a real spoiler. Not having enough of something makes us feel angry and dissatisfied with life, no matter what's showing up in the moment. What is going on could be great, but when we *believe* there isn't enough of it or enough time to enjoy it, then suddenly, we aren't enjoying it. "Not enough" takes the joy out of life. The funny thing is, the only thing that interferes with enjoying something isn't not having enough time for it, but *believing* we don't. We always have enough time for what we are doing—because we are doing it! What we might not have time for are all the other things the ego says we *should* have time for. Believing what the ego says creates the stress.

The antidote for "not enough time" is just realizing what the ego is up to. Once you see that there's always enough time—there's always enough of something that doesn't exist—then it's possible to ignore the thought that there isn't enough time. The ego makes up the idea of time and then uses that idea to tyrannize us and keep us involved with it. What better way to keep us out of the moment than the thought that there isn't enough time? That thought keeps us in the past (what we've already done) and in the future (what we still have to do), and takes us out of the present (what's going on now). It makes the present moment something we feel we have to rush through.

Believing we don't have enough time is very stressful, so people often feel they need a reward to help them recover from that stress: mindless TV watching, food, sex, or some other pleasure. The ego makes life miserable with its tyranny around time and then copes with that misery through escapism and pleasure-seeking.

You can get just as much done without this tyrannical voice, and you will enjoy it more. That voice never did a lick of work or gave you a hand with anything! It's an unpleasant commentator, creating tension and dissatisfaction. You don't need it, and you have never needed it.

The ego is all about accomplishment and doing, while Essence is about enjoying life, including work and other responsibilities, or just being. There doesn't have to be a split between work and play. Essence enjoys everything. Work and play are also concepts. The ego has difficulty enjoying either because of the concept of time. Only when we drop out of the mind and into reality (the present moment) does the sense of time disappear. Then it's possible to experience the peace that is always here, which is obscured only by the belief that it isn't here but in some other, future moment.

Just keep noticing how often the mind declares that there isn't enough of something, and know it is never true. It's a belief, a misunderstanding. It's the ego's perspective. Life is just as it needs to be right now, and it has plenty of everything that matters, such as happiness, joy, love, and peace. It's possible to discover this right now in this simple moment by just noticing that happiness, joy, love, and peace are here right now.

73: EVERYONE HAS THE SAME CAPACITY FOR ENJOYMENT

You have probably noticed how much enjoyment you can get out of the simplest little things: finding just the right candlestick for your table, potting a plant, taking a hot shower, having jeans that fit just right, or reading a book. These are things that cost very little but can deliver as much enjoyment as many things that cost much more. The myth is that there is more enjoyment in owning or doing something expensive than something less expensive. Owning or doing anything is a passing pleasure, and the pleasure of owning or doing something expensive passes just as quickly, or almost as quickly, as owning or doing something less expensive. In fact, many who are very rich get less pleasure out of their wealth than those who have little because of the law of diminishing returns. At a certain point, getting more things and better things just doesn't provide the kick it used to.

It's fun to get new things, go places, and try new things. What is interesting is that the fun isn't in what we get, where we go, or what we try as much as in just experiencing something new, and that is always possible, whether we have money or not. Everyone enjoys more and better things, but it doesn't take a huge house, a yacht, or a private airplane to enjoy life. Many people believe that those who have more are happier, but it isn't true. Everyone has the same capacity for enjoyment, and that enjoyment can come from very simple things: drinking a cup of tea on the patio on a beautiful summer morning, taking a walk in nature, listening to music, meditating, trying a new recipe, or talking with a friend.

Madison Avenue has led people to believe that having things—lots of things and lots of expensive things—will make us happier and more fulfilled, that these things mean that our life is good and successful. Quite the opposite is often true. More is not necessarily better. Having more can be worse if we believe we need those things to be happy and if we feel driven to constantly get more. This is the trap many who are rich fall into. They haven't discovered just how happy they can be with very little. That's a wonderful discovery! You can be happy with the bare essentials unless you decide you can't. If you are attached to an image of your life looking a certain way, then you will suffer if life doesn't comply. That can happen at any income level.

Madison Avenue is in the image business. It tells us what we should look like and have to be happy. These are lies, but rather insidious ones. Images from ads bypass our rational mind and go directly into our unconscious and program it. Everyone has been conditioned by these ads, and now children are being exposed to them like never before. And as you know, conditioning isn't so easy to overcome. Even those who don't want more and better things often suffer over not having what others have because striving for these things is considered normal. The pressure to have more and better things is very great in the United States and has created a stressful lifestyle that is bereft of meaning and spiritual sustenance.

When we really allow ourselves to experience life fully and enjoy the little things, life feels full and complete. Every moment has an equal potential for enjoyment, no matter what is happening. Enjoying life is really a matter of choosing to not want something other than what is here right now. Once we stop desiring more of something or something better, we begin to enjoy what is here right now.

Desiring is how the ego keeps us discontent with life and busy going after more. So much energy is wasted trying to get more and better things. It exhausts us, and it's exhausting the earth's resources. It's time to see the truth—that more things and better things don't mean more happiness or a better, more worthwhile life. For many, the pursuit of more and better things is leading to the opposite, to exhaustion and to spiritual and literal bankruptcy. All the enjoyment we need is available right now in this simple moment. As much enjoyment is possible in the present moment as in any future moment, no matter what we have or don't have and no matter what is going on.

74: EXCITEMENT

Everyone likes the feeling of being excited. It's wonderful. Excitement happens when we finally get what we want. Suddenly life is the way we (our egos) want it to be. What a relief! What happiness, when we finally get what we want! For the time being, life is good. You knew it could be that way, and now finally it is.

The trouble is that excitement, like every other feeling, comes and goes, and it can leave as quickly as it came. The ego doesn't like that. It tries to keep excitement alive as long as possible. The ego pumps up the good news or experience and tries to make it last by thinking, talking, and fantasizing about it. What will it mean in the future? How will it change my life? Exciting news or events advance the ideal story of *me*. Unpleasant or unhappy news or events do the opposite.

Some events are imbued with a lot of importance—they mean something, which is why they feel exciting. You assume they mean something about *you* ("I'm finally a success") or about *your life* ("My life is finally going to turn out"). Events become important and exciting because they are given meaning. The excitement comes from the ego getting what it wants and believing it's going to get more of what it wants.

It's a great feeling to get what we want. To the ego, it's the ultimate. Too bad that great feeling doesn't last. There's an ugly side to getting what we want, and that is the realization that getting what we want doesn't do the trick for long. The happiness and excitement don't last. We need another "fix" of getting what we want to keep the happiness and excitement going. What goes up must come down, so excitement invariably has a down side.

Disappointment, boredom, sadness, depression, or anger often follow on the heels of excitement, as the fantasies and dreams spawned by the event fail to come to pass or fail to come to pass as quickly or lavishly as hoped. The ego has a way of dreaming very big dreams that have little basis in reality.

Excitement is a sign that the ego is involved in what we are experiencing. Excitement wouldn't be present if thoughts hadn't created it: Something happened, you concluded something very positive about it, so you feel excited. Most people don't realize that their excitement comes from their positive conclusions (fantasies) and not from the event. They assume that the event caused their excitement.

That realization may seem like really bad news, at least to the ego. Sorry to rain on your parade. It's not that you should suppress your excitement if it's there, but it's helpful to become more aware of how the ego creates excitement and to become more aware of the truth about excitement—that the up becomes a down. Notice how even positive thoughts (fantasies) take you out of the moment, not just negative ones. The more you become aware of this process, the freer you become of the ego and of suffering. Freedom is better than any amount of excitement.

When you remain in the moment, events come and go, and you aren't attached to their coming or going because you aren't assigning meaning to them. You experience life as it's happening without being tossed to and fro by it. You have an experience without telling a story about it. What a relief! You just experience life without all the drama. From the place of nonattachment, every experience is good, and excitement is recognized for what it is.

75: NOTICING VS. GIVING ATTENTION

Noticing and giving attention to something are very different. When we are noticing our thoughts, we have stepped away from them and we aren't so identified with them. Noticing creates a space between our thoughts and what is experiencing thought. When we notice something, we become aligned with the Noticer, or who we really are. Then we have the opportunity to choose to give those thoughts further attention or not. This opportunity isn't available when we aren't noticing our thoughts but automatically identifying with them and responding to them, when we are so close to them that we can't see them for what they are.

Attention is more like a spotlight that focuses on something to the exclusion of everything else and gets lost in what it's focused on. When we give our attention to a thought, we become identified with it if our attention lands there long enough. Whatever we give our attention to becomes magnified in our awareness.

Noticing, on the other hand, is more like a flashlight that doesn't stay in one spot for long. When we are in Essence and noticing what we are experiencing, we are noticing lots of things. Our awareness jumps around so quickly from one thing to the next that we barely realize all the things our awareness is taking in.

Noticing is what the real you, or Essence, does as it experiences life. It gives attention to what needs attention in order to function, and then it moves on. The state of ego identification, however, is a state of giving attention to thoughts and feelings more than other aspects of experience—and believing those thoughts and feelings. Doing that colors our experience of life and interferes with experiencing life purely.

Because almost all thoughts come from the ego, if you give your attention to your thoughts, you will become identified with the ego and its perceptions. You will see life through the ego's eyes. Instead, if you give less attention to your thoughts and more attention to other aspects of life (e.g., what you are sensing, experiencing, intuiting, and being moved to do), your experience of life changes. Life seems simpler, easier, more peaceful, and less stressful.

Learning to notice thoughts without identifying with them is the key to moving out of ego identification and experiencing our true nature. Instead of being absorbed in your thoughts, take one little step back and notice what you are thinking. What you are thinking is really what your ego is thinking, not the real you.

Practice noticing your thoughts, and you can become free from the ego. Meditation is valuable because it's the practice of noticing thoughts without getting involved in them. You already know how to do this. Everyone has lots of thoughts they don't get involved in.

When you meditate, focus on something such as a sound, music, a candle flame, a mantra, bodily sensations, or your breath. Then, when you notice yourself thinking, gently bring yourself back to whatever you are meditating on. Meditation trains us to become involved in sensory experience (the real experience in the moment) instead of thoughts. You can't get rid of your thoughts, since they are beyond your control, but you can learn to just notice them and then move on to noticing what else is present in the moment.

Be careful that noticing thoughts doesn't turn into giving your attention to them because that can quickly turn into getting lost in them and ego identification. Just notice any thoughts and feelings that show up, and then turn your attention away from them and give it, instead, to anything else that's going on, and you will land in the Now.

76: ACCEPTING VS. SETTLING

When spiritual teachers suggest that we accept something, it's because it makes no sense to cling to a desire for things to be different when those things can't be changed. The only effect that such thoughts have is to make us miserable.

However, acceptance doesn't mean not doing something to try to change what you *can* change. For example, you can accept that you stubbed your toe (what good is it to complain or get angry about it?) and still do something to prevent stubbing it again. Or to use an example that may be more meaningful: If you are unhappy in your relationship, you can accept that you are unhappy and still take steps to change something within the relationship or within yourself.

Accepting a situation we don't like doesn't mean doing nothing about it. People are often afraid that if they accept a situation they don't like, they will be perpetuating it. However, acceptance isn't what perpetuates a situation but, rather, not doing something to change it. Accepting that you don't like a situation actually puts you in a better position to do something about it. On the other hand, accepting a situation that you don't like while being in denial that you don't like it is more like settling for the situation, or resigning yourself to it.

Settling for or resigning ourselves to something we don't like that we *can* change isn't the same as accepting it, because we are actually not accepting that we don't like the situation. Instead, we are pretending we like the situation so that we don't have to change anything, because that could be challenging and require some effort.

Settling feels very different from acceptance, which feels good and peaceful. Accepting that we don't like something feels much better than being in denial of the truth. Settling or resigning ourselves to something we don't like usually makes us angry, but we deny the anger and any action that might come from wanting a change, and we feel blocked, dissatisfied, and cut off from our true nature. Whenever we don't honor the movements inside of us toward greater love, growth, creativity, freedom, and peace, we remain stuck in a very uncomfortable place.

Acceptance doesn't feel like being stuck. Accepting something we don't like means also accepting that we don't like it and allowing action to happen to change that situation if that's possible. If that action comes from Essence, then taking action will be a great relief. If it comes from the ego, that action might not be ultimately satisfying, but we will probably learn from it. Acceptance isn't passive. It's an act of clear seeing, of being able to discriminate between what can and cannot be changed and acting accordingly. We accept what can't be changed and allow Essence to move us to change what can be.

77: COMPLICATIONS

The present moment is simple, uncomplicated. It's just an experience of being or existing, taking in whatever is going on, and responding naturally and spontaneously to that. This can happen with very little thought. If what we are doing requires thinking (e.g., reading, analyzing numbers, using a computer, designing, editing, planning), then the mind is part of the moment, and we use the mind as needed and put it down when we are done with it. When the ego is no longer intervening in the moment, life is very simple: no drama, no problems, no confusion, no dissatisfaction.

That simplicity can be your experience right now and in as many *nows* as you choose. Such a shift is largely a matter of seeing the truth—you don't need the egoic mind—and then choosing to be in this simple moment fully instead of absorbed in thinking about something else.

Take this simple moment that was just described and throw in some thoughts about the past, which stir up some emotions. Then throw in some thoughts about the future, which also stir up some emotions. Thoughts about the past and future complicate the moment, don't they? Now, add a few opinions. But first, you may have to consider various opinions before you decide which ones are *yours*. Opinions and beliefs aren't that simple either. They are always changing and need to be evaluated, defended, explained, expressed, and judged. Opinions and beliefs are high-maintenance. They complicate this simple moment. Do we need them? *Who* needs them? They are part of what creates the false self, or ego, which needs them to be somebody. All somebodies have opinions and beliefs, don't they?

Who you really are, Essence, doesn't *have* beliefs; it just lives its truth. Essence doesn't need to define what that is or defend it; it just follows what is true. You don't need to bring opinions and beliefs into this simple moment. They just complicate it.

And then there are desires. They seem pretty important. Don't we need desires? But aren't they just the thought "I want"? Do you need that thought to move in the world? Are those thoughts what run your life, and if they are, is that working for you? There's something else here that is running your life, if you let it, but it allows you to follow your desires and run your life that way, if you want. You don't need your desires, though. Something else is here that drives you to do what will make you happy and fulfilled. Essence's drives appear in this simple moment, unannounced and undefined. They just move you. You don't know where they will lead or why, and you don't have to know. Those drives are part of every simple moment, and they are also uncomplicated.

When the moment is stripped of the past, the future, opinions, beliefs, and desires, life becomes very simple. The ego doesn't like that, of course, because it likes complexity and drama, problems and solutions, all of which it creates. You can have the complicated life that the ego creates, or you can have an uncomplicated one, but just know that you don't have to have complications, drama, problems, or dissatisfaction. You can just be here, now, in the moment, uncluttered by thoughts about *me*, what *I* believe, *my* past and future, and what *I* want. You really don't need any of them.

78: WANTING MEANING

Meaning is inherent in life—life is meaningful. However, wanting meaning is just one more desire to suffer over. While meaning comes from Essence, the desire for meaning comes from the ego. We only desire what we feel is lacking, and the ego is what experiences lack and therefore desires. The ego doesn't experience the meaning inherent in any moment, so it desires it. The ego is out of touch with meaning, so it desires meaning. When we are identified with the ego, we are always looking for something to satisfy what is never satisfied—the ego. And meaning is just one more thing the ego seeks, when meaning is right in front of the ego's nose.

Meaning is right here, right now in the experience—the gift—of life. Being alive is meaningful, and whatever springs out of this moment is meaningful. Life feels meaningful when we are in touch with Essence and Essence's experience of life. The ego, however, is looking for something more, as usual, something that will make the ego feel meaningful. The ego isn't necessarily looking for the experience of meaning, which is already here.

"What will make me and my life meaningful?" asks the ego. The ego wants to be meaningful and wants its life to be meaningful. "To whom?" we have to ask. The ego wants its life to be meaningful to *others* so that it is cherished, loved, and admired, which is also why it wants a lot of other things. Wanting meaning is a form of spiritual ego. It's a higher desire, not as materialistic as wanting a new car, but ultimately the ego's desire for meaning is still in service to enhancing its self-image, and the ego imagines that it will feel better about itself once and for all if it finally finds meaning.

The trouble is the ego looks for meaning in all the wrong places. It looks for meaning in accomplishments and experiences. But these come and go, and the ego never has enough accomplishments and experiences to be satisfied. The ego experiences meaning briefly from these, and then it's back to lacking meaning, to needing more meaning. The one place the ego doesn't look for meaning is in the beauty of the present moment. It doesn't expect to find it there, so it looks everywhere else. How can there be meaning in just existing? This makes no sense to the ego. To it, only a fool or a child could be satisfied with that. The ego overlooks the one thing that can satisfy—the present moment.

It should be no surprise that the ego discounts the present moment, since the ego disappears when we drop into the moment. The ego is just thoughts about ourselves and our life, and when we are no longer engaged with such thoughts, but involved in the experience of our being existing in this moment, the ego (the sense of I) vanishes. The ego can't experience true meaning because as soon as we do, the ego dissolves.

Only when you drop out of your egoic mind and into Essence can you experience true meaning, and in that experience nothing else is needed, nothing is missing or lacking. What a relief it is to experience true meaning. You didn't have to strive and struggle for it after all. It was here all along, only hidden by the ego that told you it wasn't here and that you had to go searching for it.

And so it is with the spiritual search as well: We think we have to seek enlightenment, when all we really have to do is just allow ourselves to be here right now in this moment without seeking, trying, striving, wanting, needing, doubting, fearing, judging, or doing any of the other things the ego tells us we have to do to be happy and safe. The ego is a liar, and once you stop believing it, you find everything you were looking for.

79: ABOUT EFFORT

Whether something we do is effort*ful* or effort*less* depends on where the motivation to do it comes from. Whenever doing comes from the ego, from a thought, such as, "I have to do this" or "I should do this," those efforts will feel effortful and be characterized by trying and striving. On the other hand, when doing comes from Essence, it isn't motivated by a thought, but by a drive or urge to act that has joy, excitement, and a feeling of "yes" attached to it.

The difference between effortful, ego-driven activity and effortless activity is joy. Efforts that come out of joy are easeful, spontaneous, fluid, and effortless; while efforts that come out of conditioning or "shoulds" are generally accompanied by tension, stress, confusion, resentment, anger, fear, resistance—and desires.

Another difference is that effortful activity isn't done for itself, for the joy of doing it, but to get or avoid something. Although Essence-driven efforts may have a goal, the pursuit of that goal is intrinsically rewarding and results in happiness, fulfillment, excitement, and joy. Ego-driven efforts, on the other hand, are often not enjoyed, but endured for the promise of a reward or to avoid some negative consequence or something feared. The journey to the goal isn't enjoyed, life is not enjoyed.

When we aren't enjoying life, we are in the grip of the ego. When we are enjoying it, we are either engaged in activity that is aligned with Essence or in touch with Essence by simply being present to whatever we are doing. What a wonderful world this is, that joy is a signpost that points us in the right direction. How wonderful that the prescription for a happy life is to follow our joy, and not the opposite.

People often act like the opposite is true, as if doing what they don't want to do is the key to happiness and fulfillment. The ego's goals require unpleasant efforts, struggle, striving, stress, and strain. People think these efforts are necessary to finally, one day, be happy. They sacrifice the happiness that comes from simply being present to what is here right now and from moving as Essence would in hopes of a happier future, which never comes. The ego doesn't deliver on its promises of happiness. It only keeps pushing us toward its superficial goals and some imagined future, all the while making us miserable.

Striving is the experience of trying to get something that isn't here right now. When people finally get what they've been striving for, they usually keep on striving for something else that isn't here right now. There's no end to the things that aren't here right now, so there's no end to striving if we buy into the idea that we need something other than the joy of simply existing and responding to life from our true nature before we can be happy.

When people hear this message, they are afraid if they stop striving that nothing will get done and their life will fall apart. It's true that the ego's goals may suffer, but the life that comes out of following your joy will be much happier and more productive in meaningful ways. You will be motivated by your inner joy to develop your talents, express your creativity, serve others, learn, grow, unfold yourself in meaningful ways, and take time for love and to enjoy life. You won't lack drive; it will just be coming from a deeper place and lead to more meaningful accomplishments. There will probably be plenty of doing, but it will be balanced by just being and connecting with Essence and with those you love.

Nothing of value is lost in not allowing the ego to determine where your energies go. Something else much wiser will take its place, something that has been trying to guide your life all along.

80: IT'S ALL ABOUT PERSPECTIVE

Making things more important than they are is one way the ego keeps us out of the present moment. This is particularly apparent when something truly significant happens, like when we or someone close to us nearly dies or experiences a crisis. Crises and death put the other things the ego magnifies in importance into perspective. The ego doesn't have perspective, which is one reason we suffer when we are identified with it. Its perspective is narrow: Life is good when we are getting what it wants and bad when we aren't.

The trouble is the ego's desires aren't a good guide for what is important in life or for what will make us happy. And the ego often overlooks what might really make us happy, such as taking time to just be, connect with loved ones, or do something fun or creative. The ego tends to drive us to achieve, improve ourselves, and get more things. While there is obviously a place for doing those things, focusing exclusively on what the ego wants can leave us feeling empty, disconnected from life, exhausted, and never having or being enough.

The ego tells us that we have to have certain things or be a certain way to be happy, and it's wrong—we don't. It also assumes that every step in its plan for happiness has to work out or the plan will be ruined, and we will never be happy. Every little difficulty we encounter is felt to be proof of failure and a reason to be unhappy rather than a natural part of the process of life unfolding. Every action and event is examined from the standpoint of whether it will get the ego what it wants or interfere with that. The ego has many goals, and it sees events in life as either helping or hindering it toward those goals. If something helps, that's good, and a happy life seems possible. If something hinders, that's bad, and a failed and unhappy life is assumed to be our destiny.

The suffering begins with an evaluation of something as good or bad, followed by a story of what that will mean: being a success or failure, being happy or unhappy, being loved or lonely, having ease or having to struggle, being rich or being poor. The ego thinks in terms of black and white, never shades of gray, and life just isn't like that. The ego's reality is black and white, but real reality is messy, complex, unpredictable, and no one story we can tell about it is true. The ego doesn't like that, of course. It likes its stories of good and bad, and the drama and suffering they cause. It likes its stories because they give it a false sense of security, a sense of knowing how life is. The ego isn't looking for truth; it just wants a story it can believe so that it can pretend it knows how and where life is going.

The ego is in the business of creating suffering because suffering keeps us tied to the ego and allows the ego to exist. If you stopped suffering, you would no longer be identified with the ego, and it would stop existing. You would stop experiencing yourself as the *me* who has this problem and that problem, this desire and that goal, this self-image, and that past. The ego only exists as a story about *you*. Nothing else. So that story better be a dramatic one, or we will lose interest and drop out of our mind and into the present moment, where the ego disappears.

The ego has quite a racket going: It makes even small things a life and death matter to keep us involved with it. If something is important and it's going wrong, which is the ego's basic story, then we'd better pay attention to the ego's solution for fixing it, or we will really have a problem. The ego keeps our attention with its stories, with dealing with the feelings those stories cause, and with the actions needed to make those stories turn out better. Yes, it has quite a racket going.

Meanwhile, life is happening in its own way and in its own time, and we are missing out on what is really going on because we are busy trying to make life turn out the way the ego wants. Most people's lives are about getting their story to turn out the way they want, regardless of what the Intelligence behind life might have in mind. People suffer so much when their ego's desires don't match what life brings them, and that suffering is so unnecessary. The ego's desires are created by the ego. Why build your life around them, when something much deeper is at play, living and directing your life? You might miss what Essence is moving you to do if you are too busy being moved by the ego.

You can live your life as the ego intends or as Essence intends, and most people's lives are a combination of the two. Paying attention to the ego's stories and what's important to it, however, often brings a lot of pain. The ego tells sad and scary stories most of the time, and if you listen to it, you will organize your life to ward off what the ego fears instead of enjoying the life Essence can create through you.

To the ego, life is a battle it's trying to win, and every little difficulty feels like a threat to its self-image, life, and happiness. But that is its perspective. To Essence, life is an experience to be enjoyed, an opportunity for exploration, discovery, growth, love, and service. Who is there to battle with? The ego tilts at windmills. When we know ourselves as the Oneness, it's a friendly universe, where we welcome and accept challenges (including the challenge of having an ego), not as our enemy, but as our friend, or at least our teacher.

When we are happy and aligned with Essence, the unimportant, small things in life stay small. They are seen in proper perspective.

Essence gives us back our perspective, which is a very good reason to align with it rather than the ego. When we do, life becomes easier, not because anything has changed, but because our perspective has.

81: YOUR FAVORITE THINGS

What do you like most about being alive now on planet earth? The song from "The Sound of Music" about favorite things ("Raindrops on roses and whiskers on kittens... these are a few of my favorite things") is an expression from Essence. When we are in Essence, we love the little things, like whiskers on kittens—what a miracle! There's so much joy when we are really present to life and the miracle that it is. We get joy from the littlest things.

This is so unlike the ego, which disparages such things. "Oh that—I've seen that before!" is its attitude. It wants life to be about *it*, not about life itself. The ego loves whatever makes it feel good about *itself*, not what makes it feel good. This egocentricity is one of the most obvious differences between the state of ego identification and our natural state, or Essence. The ego refers whatever is happening back to itself: What will it mean to *me*? But when we are in Essence, we experience Essence's joy at experiencing itself through *all* of creation.

So what is it you love about life? It's so good to notice and acknowledge this because doing so aligns us with Essence and strengthen our awareness of Essence's presence in our life. When we notice those whiskers, those dew drops, those beautiful and amazing things about planet earth and its creations, we can't help but feel Essence's joy. The only thing that gets in the way of that joy is not noticing such things, and the only reason we don't is if we are busy noticing something else, which for most people is their thoughts.

Do your thoughts bring you that same kind of joy? It really helps to notice the impact that thoughts have on your state of consciousness because when you do, you see that they don't give you the same peace, joy, and happiness that noticing life more purely does.

Do you love how the clouds move and shift as you watch them? Do you love how the stars seem to twinkle? Do you love how your dog's chest moves up and down when breathing? Do you love the sound of the wind in the trees before a storm? Do you love the smell of damp leaves in the fall? Do you love the feel of the water against your skin when you are swimming through it? It's impossible to run out of things to love about life. What a wonderful spiritual practice it is to notice and feel gratitude for the little things in life. What feels that way is Essence. So you see, Essence is very close at hand. It's not some mysterious force separate from us, but that which lives through us and experiences this precious life we have been given.

What a different world it is when, instead, we are identified with the ego. Every little experience and change has tension around it: Will it be good or bad for *me?* The ego evaluates everything, even the breeze, even the dew, even the whiskers on kittens. It can find a problem with anything: The breeze musses *my* hair, the dew makes *my* feet wet, *I* need to trim those whiskers. That's how the ego sees life. It's always about how something affects *me,* how it might affect *me* in the future, or how it has affected *me* in the past.

The egoic mind tells stories about the big and little things in life, which takes us out of the experience of life and makes life seem more terrible, frightening, and troublesome than it actually is. The reason living in Essence feels peaceful is that peace is the real experience of life. Yes, life is more peaceful than the ego's experience of it. The mind scares us and causes us to distrust life and live in fear, doubt, and suspicion of what is going to happen rather than in excited anticipation for what will be revealed next in this great adventure called life. Yes, life is terrible sometimes, but it's never as terrible as the mind says it is. The ego makes it terrible by telling us it is terrible. How obvious this is once we really look, and that is the difference. When we are conscious and noticing what's true rather than unconscious and accepting what the mind tells us, the truth is obvious. Just notice this beautiful gift of life you have been given. Just notice what is true and real.

82: APPLES AND ORANGES

The mind is useful in making distinctions between things, finding differences, and evaluating them. The ego loves to use that mental capacity to compare things and people. It loves numbers because they seem to give it a clear way of knowing where it, others, and other things stand—what or who is better. The ego loves the ten-scale for that reason, and it's always seeking to be a ten or have something or someone who is a ten. The ego is just as happy to bask in reflected glory.

The mind uses comparisons to make wise, practical decisions: It chooses an apple that isn't bruised over a bruised one. However, the egoic mind compares people in the same way the mind compares things. Comparing an apple to another apple is one thing, but comparing a person to another person is like comparing an apple to an orange. Such comparisons aren't useful. They are false. And when we compare ourselves to others, we always suffer, whether we come out on top or not.

Making comparisons is one of the ego's favorite ways of causing suffering. It looks for ways we fall short so that we feel we have a problem, and then it offers a solution. In this way, the ego keeps us tied to thoughts about how to improve ourselves and our life. It keeps us very busy this way and involved with thoughts about ourselves. We are the ego's project, and it takes this self-improvement project very seriously.

Notice how often your egoic mind compares you with others. It does it immediately and automatically whenever it encounters someone. This is part of everyone's programming. Once we realize that doing this is just our programming and that it only causes us suffering, we can more easily ignore this aspect of ourselves that loves to compare. It isn't that difficult to ignore this programming. Comparing ourselves with others or comparing others with others is a habit that can be broken just by seeing how untrue and useless such comparisons are.

Nothing actually compares to something else because everything is unique, even every apple is unique. While there may be some usefulness in comparing an apple to another apple, there's no usefulness in doing that with people. The ego pretends to be helpful by doing this with people, but such comparisons only serve the ego, which is attempting to see itself as superior or find a way to get to the top. These attempts to be, or just feel, superior leave us feeling bad. Feeling superior, especially by tearing others down, is definitely not a route to happiness, although the ego believes it is.

Feeling happy and good about ourselves comes from being in Essence, which is a state of unity with others and life, not separation. We are happiest when we drop into the flow of life and are responding naturally to it without the interference, judgments, confusion, and complications of the egoic mind. The ego separates us from others, and listening to it removes us from real life. The ego doesn't know how to make us happy, or even successful. Giving power over to the ego is like giving the steering wheel to a child. The ego doesn't know how to get us where we really want to go, even though it pretends to.

Comparing people is as ridiculous as the following conversation:

"Apples are better than oranges because you don't have to peel them."

"No, oranges are better than apples because they're juicier."

"Apples are better than oranges because red is prettier than orange."

"Oranges are better than apples because they are already in sections for eating."

"Apples are better than oranges because they are crunchy."

"Oranges are better than apples because you don't have to wash them."

You get the picture. The trouble with comparing people, as with oranges and apples, is not only that comparisons are often subjective and reflect a personal preference (e.g., "Red is prettier than orange"), but also that concluding that something or someone is better based on one feature is ridiculous. How can anyone take into account or even know all the qualities of another human being, and whose to say one characteristic is better than another? The ego, of course, is what thinks this way, and it will look for something in others that will make us feel either less than or superior because that is its objective. That's what its comparisons are really all about.

Once we have seen how faulty the ego's thinking is and how false comparisons are, we can be done with that way of thinking and the suffering it causes ourselves and others. Oranges are wonderful, apples are wonderful, we are wonderful, and so is everyone else. Let's just leave it at that and enjoy whatever is in front of us. Why waste this precious moment on comparisons? What's left is simply gratitude for the uniqueness of every little thing in life. What a miracle!

83: WE ARE EXPLORERS

Everyone is entirely unique. No one sees through the same eyes. Because everyone's consciousness is different, everyone has a unique experience of life. What a mystery consciousness is! And that's how it's meant to be. We, as individuated "sparks" of the Creator, have differentiated to give the Creator a unique experience. Every person lives in his or her own world, his or her own consciousness, and has a unique experience of life. We can never really know what someone else's consciousness is like.

Just as the Creator is enjoying exploring different places in consciousness, or states of consciousness, through each of us, we get to explore, or experience, to some extent other people's consciousness by knowing them intimately or by experiencing their creations. What we love so much about movies, stories, music, and art is that we get to experience, as much as we can, someone else's consciousness—how someone else sees and experiences the world and how someone else feels. We get to try on for size the characters in a movie or novel for a little while. We live a million lives vicariously through movies, stories, and other creative experiences. We see through a million other eyes and bodies. What an amazing thing it is to experience something beyond our own experience.

Some people and their expressions resonate with us (we like where their consciousness takes us), and some don't (we don't like where their consciousness takes us). We generally gravitate toward people and artistic expressions that move us into a state of consciousness we enjoy, or at least find interesting to explore temporarily, although sometimes we like to have an experience just because it's different or because we like to be stretched, even though the experience may not be enjoyable. Other people are really a gift to us in this way—a gift the Oneness gives itself, really.

The ability to experience other people's consciousness by being close to them or by experiencing their creative expressions is one of the things that's so fun about life, and the Creator thinks so too! We are microcosms of the Oneness: It explores consciousness through us, and we also explore consciousness through others and their creations. The ego may want people to be a certain way or to be similar to it, but who we really are—the Oneness—wants to experience all kinds and levels of consciousness. And through contact with the beautiful array of ways of being, each consciousness is changed.

We are supposed to be different—this life is an exploration. We aren't supposed to be exploring the same state of consciousness as someone else, and it would be impossible to do that anyway because each body-mind is unique and so is the place and time in which each of us exists. Our egos often try hard to be like someone else, but we were never meant to be like anyone else, although we are meant to influence each other. That makes the game all the more fun and interesting.

What a delight! We are here to learn, grow, and evolve, and all this growth can be fun—and is fun. Notice what a good time you are having discovering how you see things and how everyone else is doing life.

84: WHY TELL A STORY?

Every experience you have ever had is in the past. It's gone and will never be here again. All you have left is a memory, and a memory is but a shadow of the actual experience, a weak, faded remembrance with lots of gaps. A memory, in fact, is not an experience at all, but a thought, which is why memories are not as fulfilling as experiences. As soon as we put a memory into words and tell a story about it, we are no longer in the *memory*, but in the *story* of the past, which are two very different things. A memory is information stored as an image, while a story is a point of view. A story is much narrower than an actual memory, since it includes much less information than a memory. Certain pieces of information are selected from a memory to include in the story, and the rest is left out, including the various perspectives of those present. A story about the past can only be one point of view.

When we tell a story about the past, that story is our point of view, which then seems to be the true story (because people like to believe their own perspective). Telling a story about the past solidifies the past and makes the story seem true. And the more we tell that story, the truer it seems. The actual memory that the story is based on fades or is forgotten, and all we are left with is our story, which we remember because we have repeated it so many times. We become convinced of our story (we've convinced ourselves of it) and attached to it because it's ours, so then we feel compelled to repeat it, defend it, convince others of it, and make sure it remains true, even if it causes us pain. It becomes our "truth," which really just means our ego's truth.

The trouble with stories is that they aren't neutral, at least not for long, because stories are told by the ego, and the ego always has an agenda. It wants to either paint us as superior or reinforce its negative identities, and it likes to create drama and problems to solve. So although we can recount something about the past in a neutral way (e.g., "I ran into my ex-husband in the grocery store last week"), give it a moment, and the ego is bound to tack on its spin, just to add a little drama, make us right, or uphold our identities (e.g., "He looked terrible. I don't think he's doing well. He never should have left me"). Talking about the past in a neutral way might serve some informational purpose if we were able to do that; however, most conversations about the past have the ego's spin on them, which results in feelings we are left to deal with.

So here's the problem: When you tell stories about the past, you are bound to create feelings. And since it's the ego spinning the stories, the feelings aren't likely to be good ones. People struggle so much with the past, not because the past was necessarily so awful, but because the ego's story about the past makes them feel bad. Then those feelings are experienced as a problem. People are often angry about what happened in the past because their stories about it make them angry and prevent them from enjoying life now. But it doesn't have to be that way.

The past isn't the problem. When we stop telling stories about the past, the past stops being a problem. Memories of the past don't create negative feelings. Memories are just stored information. It is stories about the past that create negative feelings. This is really good news because it means we aren't doomed to unhappiness because of something that happened in the past. Leave the past in the past, stop telling the stories you've been telling about the past, forget them, and live your life now, free of all stories.

The way to get free of your stories is by seeing that you are telling stories and by noticing the impact that doing so has on your consciousness and happiness. If you want to be happy more than you want your stories, you will give up your stories, because why would you want to be unhappy when you don't have to be?

85: LIVING WITH UNCERTAINTY

We live in a state of uncertainty. You may be certain about some things, but the overall experience in any moment is one of uncertainty: What will happen? Why did that happen? Why is this happening? When will it be over? What will be the result? These questions are our constant companions in life. We are doomed to uncertainty, or so the ego feels. That's not the experience of Essence, however, which enjoys the uncertainty of life. Essence isn't what asks those questions. The ego poses them and tries to answer them to try to gain some sense of control over life, which is essentially uncontrollable, unpredictable, and unknown.

Let's take a look at some of these questions, because people tend to think they are valid and valuable, but really, they belong to the ego and its way of thinking and are related to its desires and fears. The desire for life to be a certain way and the fear that it won't be drive those questions and every other activity of the ego. The problem with these questions is they presume an overly simplistic answer: What will happen? This will happen. End of story. Why is this happening? Because of this. End of story. When will it be over? Time and date. End of story. What will be the result? This will. End of story.

None of those questions can be answered so simply. It can't even be said when something will be over. At what point is an experience actually over? When some event is over or when our tension around it is over or when something else about it is over? What does "over" mean, anyway? "Over" is a concept, not a reality. And "Why?" is a question people ask all the time, but it rarely has a simple answer. There are many reasons why something happens, many of which can never be known. Why is part of the great mystery of life, and we rarely ever learn the whole truth. This fact is hard for the ego to swallow.

The mind wants answers to those unanswerable questions because it thinks it will finally be able to relax and accept life once it has them, but relaxation and acceptance aren't dependent on answers. They result from a choice you make right now about your relationship to life: Will you relax and go with and accept the flow of life right now or not? Will you say yes to life right now, no matter what is happening, or not? Will you be present to what is happening instead of complaining about it or dreaming of something else?

Paradoxically, being able to be present and accept life actually depends on being willing to not know the answer to those questions! Saying yes to life is a lot easier if we aren't presuming something false or negative, which is generally the result of believing the ego's answers to the unanswerable questions in life.

The ego's answers to these questions—why something is happening or has happened, what it means, what will happen—are made up and actually take us away from the very happiness and peace we are searching for. The ego's conclusions are often negatively slanted and erroneous. They are too narrow and short-sighted to be the whole story. The ego often answers those questions pessimistically and with little wisdom, so we are left with a bleak vision, which can make us feel unhappy and discontent. The ego tells us a bad and sad story, and we believe it and take it to be the truth. And since we can never know if its conclusions are right, we often go round and round mentally, adopting one conclusion and then another. That takes a lot of energy and attention away from being present in our life, which is the real source of happiness.

Life is much wiser than the ego. It's wise and good and can be trusted. So even if you don't know why things are happening or have happened or what will happen, everything that happens is taking you back Home to Essence, toward being the loving and wise being that you really are. That's all you need to know. When knowing that is enough, you land in a place where all is well and always has been. And that's what you have wanted all along, not certainty or answers.

86: WHO AM I TO JUDGE?

First of all, "Who am I?" is an excellent question to ponder because, as many of you know, the *you* that you think you are is just thoughts *about* you. These thoughts about ourselves are called the ego, and they give us a sense of existing as an individual. The ego has a lot of thoughts about everything else as well, particularly in the form of judgments, conclusions, opinions, evaluations, preferences, and desires. The *you* is very convincing! It has everything but a face, although it has an image of itself, lots of images in fact. Our physical body is the vehicle that the Being we are is inhabiting, so the ego can't really claim it.

The favorite activity of the conglomeration of thoughts called the ego is to judge. From its judgments come conclusions, opinions, preferences, and desires, which give rise to feelings, responses, and actions. That is how the illusion of *you* is perpetuated, simply through thoughts, including desires, that lead to feelings, responses, and actions.

What would happen if you pulled the plug on those thoughts, if you stopped believing them, stopped giving them your attention? We have an innate fear around doing this. It feels like if we were to stop thinking and believing our thoughts, we wouldn't survive or wouldn't survive well, and it's true that the ego won't survive this. Not believing our thoughts feels very dangerous. But what you discover when you stop believing them is that the real you is alive and well and living this life regardless of these thoughts. Who you really are is seeing out of your eyes, breathing, doing, and sometimes even speaking. It even uses the mind from time to time when it needs to for practical matters. You could say that it cohabitates with the ego, or false self, and allows us to believe we are the false self.

When we stop believing that our thoughts are *our* thoughts and realize that they are the conditioning our body-mind was given, most of which is not useful and leads to suffering, we have the opportunity to discover who we really are, and who we really are has no judgments whatsoever. Good and bad, ugly and pretty, smart and dumb, and every other dichotomy the ego uses to judge are concepts created by the ego for its purposes. Such concepts have some practical value, but not in the way the ego uses them. It uses them to make itself superior and to pretend to know things, as a way of tricking us into believing it. There's a reason the ego is called the false self! What it offers is mostly untrue.

One way to cut through to the true self is to see this about judgment. When you catch yourself involved in judging or telling a story about something, ask, "Who am I to judge (or make that conclusion)"? That question moves us out of the ego's know-it-all stance and into a more humble relationship with life, which is far too mysterious for the mind to understand. We can never and will never understand life, so why pretend? The truth is there's so much we don't know, so we are in no position to judge or draw conclusions. Acknowledging that aligns us with Essence.

"Who am I to judge?" brings us back into our true and natural relationship with life, which is one of mystery and wonder. Not having the weight of judging or knowing on our shoulders is such a relief. What a responsibility it is to pass judgment. Judges in our courts have to study many years and have lots of experience, and still they do their job imperfectly. What are the ego's credentials? What makes it qualified to judge? It's not, of course. No one is. So admit the truth and let life be as it is and let yourself be part of the mystery that life is.

87: TRUSTING WHAT IS

If life is a manifestation of Oneness (and it is), then anything that is manifest is of God, or the Oneness. Manifestation comes out of the Oneness' love of creation. The Oneness loves to create, and it loves its creations. Whatever exists is part of creation, no matter what it is, even negative thoughts and feelings. Nothing is left out; everything must be part of it. The ego, which generates negativity, is a creation of the Oneness and serves the Oneness in doing what it does. It may be difficult from our perspective to appreciate how the ego, which is selfish and causes so much trouble, suffering, and harm, can be beloved by the Creator, but the ego is the Creator's tool, a means of exploring life through the polarity of positive and negative. The ego provides the negative pole in this world.

The Creator gains much from getting lost in its creations and in the ego, just as we do. When we are lost in an unloving perspective, as we are when we are identified with the ego, we appreciate love all the more when we find it. The dark allows us to appreciate the light. How better to develop an appreciation of love than to experience a lack of it? The Truth is known by experiencing its opposite, at least in this world.

Because life is designed to teach love, whatever happens to us, including our negative thoughts and feelings, can be trusted to do that, however farfetched that may seem. The ego creates the pain around being alive, and it blames life for that pain. We are meant to see through this deception, to see that pain is part of life and that pain leads to love, not necessarily to more suffering unless we choose to blame life for the pain and not see our role in creating that pain by what we believe and think. This is an upside-down world, where believing our thoughts takes us to hell (suffering) and not believing our thoughts takes us to heaven (peace). Our salvation is in discovering that what we have assumed to be true is, in fact, false. Life is a mystery, and the mystery is solved by not thinking like everyone else (as is so often the case in mystery stories) or, in this case, by not thinking at all.

What sets humanity apart from other creatures is our ability to reason and make choices based on what we know. This is a marvelous gift, and thinking has greatly advanced our species. However, the egoic mind is an aspect of the mind that is a holdover from more primitive times. It's irrational rather than rational. It destroys rather than uplifts. It's the enemy of the intellect and reason, unlike the more functional aspect of mind that we reason with. The egoic mind is quite contrary to progress and unable to move beyond the past and see truly. It is devoid of wisdom and objectivity.

Fortunately, we are innately wise, although that wisdom isn't experienced through the mind, but through the Heart, as a deep knowing that comes from the Intelligence that we are. That we are never actually separate from the Oneness and its love and wisdom, even though the ego gives us that impression, is proof of the benevolence behind all life.

This benevolent Intelligence is who we really are, even as we inhabit these human bodies. That is the great gift we have been given as sentient beings: We are aware of our true nature, or can be, like perhaps no other creature on earth. It is our destiny to know that, to discover that. And the ego, by taking us away from our true nature, actually serves to show us that. The pain of being divorced from our true nature drives us to rediscover it. We can trust life to show us our true nature because life was specifically designed to do so.

Life is trustworthy because the Intelligence behind it is trustworthy. This Intelligence has never used punishment to teach us. We may assume that unpleasant events are a punishment from God for something, but such assumptions are the ego's ignorant stories, which only take us away from the truth and make us suffer. Teaching and learning *are* occurring, but not through punishment, but through carefully designed circumstances, which is what karma is.

There is only Goodness, and that goodness is trustworthy. It's not cruel, although we may project cruelty onto events we don't like. Death, illness, and calamities are part of life, but they aren't cruel. They aren't personal. They are just part of life and part of being human. They aren't proof of an unjust, cruel, or uncaring God. Life is as it is. Our divinity enjoys it as it is, while our ego rails against it. The more you are able to align within you with that which loves life and ignore that which doesn't, the less you will suffer and the more you will live in joy. Life is benevolent in creating a reality where suffering points us away from suffering.

88: WELCOME TO MY WORLD

When people say "Welcome to my world," what they mean is "Welcome to the way I'm experiencing life. This is what it feels like to be me. This is my reality." That phrase expresses so beautifully the truth that our reality is subjective—our reality is our *experience* of reality or of our situation, no one else's. That reality is created not only by the choices we and others make, but also by what we tell ourselves about our situation—the stories we tell or, rather, our egoic mind tells.

When people describe their life, they tell us their perception of it, which isn't the truth. No one person's perception could be the truth, although it feels like the truth to that person. It's their reality, and they often don't realize they are telling a story that affects how they experience life. They just think they are experiencing the situation, without realizing they are experiencing the effects of what they are telling themselves about it.

The stories we tell about our life color our experience of life. They don't necessarily create or change the circumstances we find ourselves in, although they might, but they certainly affect how we experience our circumstances. Any situation can be experienced as terrible or not, depending on what we tell ourselves about it. Even something that would generally be considered great could be experienced as terrible if we tell ourselves something scary about it. The situation doesn't determine our experience of it; the stories we tell about it do.

This is a powerful and life-altering realization. When it's said that we create our reality, it means, in part, that we create our *experience* of life by how we think about it. We create our mental world, and that mental world affects how we experience our situation and, moreover, also how we respond to it. Our responses to our situation then impact the situation further and affect how others respond to us and how available certain opportunities are. We do certain things in response to our perceptions, and those actions create reactions from others, more experiences, more stories, and more feelings. We create our inner reality by the stories we tell, and that inner reality creates, in part, our outer reality.

We can get off the wheel of ego-generated activity by not believing the thoughts that limit us and by seeing that our perceptions and stories don't have to be what determines our actions and experience of life. Instead, we can respond naturally, purely, to life as it arises, without these stories.

Living this way leaves us with much less to do because stories create unpleasant feelings that become a problem to be dealt with, either internally or by taking action, all of which could have been avoided if the stories hadn't been believed. The trouble with stories is they are often negative and therefore often lead to negative feelings and misguided actions, and that can only mean more trouble. Stories complicate and clutter life unnecessarily, and they create suffering.

So what does "your world" look like? If someone stepped into it, what would he or she experience? Do you like it? If not, do you realize you can change it? Drop your stories, and your experience of life will change. And when your experience of life changes, you will find yourself doing different things and responding differently to people. Without our stories, we still have a life; it's just no longer shaped by the negativity in our mind. Then when you say, "Welcome to my world," it won't be said with sarcasm, but with joy.

89: ESCAPISM

Many people feel the need to escape their life. But often what they really want to escape from is their thoughts *about* their life: their fears, worries, negative self-images, desires, judgments, and the ego's discontentment with and resistance to life. Many have lives that are perfectly acceptable and potentially happy, but they create unhappiness and stress by how they think about themselves, others, their life, and life in general. For most people, the problem isn't their life, but their thoughts about it. Even a mind that isn't particularly negative can be annoying and exhausting because of the way minds tend to spin around and around and rarely shut off.

Escape from our egoic mind happens successfully at night, so that's one very important and necessary way we refresh ourselves. Waking up from sleep is an opportunity to see how we create our sense of self and experience of life with our thoughts. There's a moment just after we wake up when we are in touch with our true nature, just before we remember who we *think* we are and what we *think* our problems are.

People often seek escape from the rattling on of their minds through alcohol, drugs, TV, food, sex, adventure, sports, hobbies, and other forms of entertainment. These things that bring a sense of relief don't change our life, but merely remove us from involvement in thoughts about it and how it's going. Television and movies give us a glimpse of other people's minds, which is one way of getting a break from our story and the usual train of thoughts. Drugs and alcohol, on the other hand, actually alter conscious in such a way that our usually way of thinking is different, not always improved, but at least different.

Television and movies may not shift consciousness, depending on the program we are watching, but the break they give us from our own thoughts has some value. However, when television or the movies reinforce our fears or other negative conditioning, as they do sometimes, they aren't ultimately helpful. Television and movies are often a way the egoic mind becomes reconditioned or that conditioning is reinforced. Although television and movies have a short-term benefit of providing relief from our own stories and other thoughts, they are often detrimental in the long term unless they uplift, inspire, open the Heart, educate, or heal, which some certainly do. Television and movies can be quite the force for raising consciousness, but unfortunately, many TV programs and movies further entrap us in egoic consciousness.

Some people are living lives that don't fit for them or that aren't conducive to happiness. Many cope with that by escaping through drugs, alcohol, or other addictions. In these cases, life doesn't need to be escaped, but changed, and acknowledging their unhappiness rather than trying to escape from it in these ways would help these individuals become motivated to make the necessary changes. Escaping when changes need to be made is a dysfunctional way of dealing with the need for change.

On the other hand, escaping the ego's story by becoming involved in things we enjoy or things that shift our consciousness, such as sports, hobbies, meditation, dancing, singing, chanting, listening to and playing music, being alone in nature, being creative, playing, and other activities is healthy rather than dysfunctional. Being involved in the ego to the exclusion of Essence is dysfunctional, although that isn't necessarily recognized by our own egos or by society.

Whatever activities bring us in touch with our own inner joy is a spiritual practice of sorts and a necessary balance to the amount of time most of us spend involved with the egoic mind. Cultivate healthy ways of leaving your mind behind—creativity, meditation, play, absorption in a sport or hobby, dancing, music, singing, praying, being in nature—and you won't need to indulge in less healthy ways.

When you do spend more time in activities that support Essence, you come to see that the egoic mind isn't who you are, and whatever it's saying has nothing to do with who you really are. You become able to experience yourself apart from your mind as easily as you experience yourself apart from someone else's mind. From that place, it becomes clear what life wants of you and what changes, if any, are necessary to lead a more fulfilled life, one you won't need to escape from.

90: HAPPINESS IS BEING IN THE PRESENT MOMENT

Love naturally flows out of the present moment, which is the only moment that exists. The present moment is what is real. When we bring a memory from the past, a fantasy of the future, a fear, a judgment, or any other self-centered thought into the present moment, those thoughts draw us out of the present-moment reality, where love and the potential for happiness exist, and into the ego's world, which is a world of discontentment, judgment, striving, and desiring. All of the pain in the world is created by identifying with such thoughts. The antidote for this pain is simply moving into the present moment and out of our thoughts about life, about ourselves, and about others.

One of the main ways suffering is created is by hanging on to the past by thinking about it and telling stories about it. We hang on to painful events at least as much as we try to hang on to happy memories, even though there is nothing left to hang on to. The past is gone, and all we have is a memory of it—a thought. Is a thought the past? Can a thought change the past or re-create the past? No. A thought is impotent, powerless. But it's worse than that: When you bring a memory of the past into the present moment, your experience of the present moment is changed. You are no longer experiencing life purely, but colored by either the pain of the past or the longing for the past. When you do this, you won't be able to experience the joy, love, and peace that are available in the present moment.

When we are fully in the present moment instead of absorbed in our thoughts about the past or the future or thoughts about ourselves and how our life is going, life feels good, we feel happy and at peace. However, if we bring thoughts into this moment that cause us to feel unhappy and discontent with the present moment, we won't experience that inherent happiness and peace. We will think that our life isn't good, that happiness isn't available, when it is.

Thoughts create our unhappiness, not circumstances. This is one of life's great secrets. It's a secret because it seems like the opposite is true—that if we could just get circumstances to change, we would finally be happy. But that just isn't true. Happiness is a potential in any moment, and it is what we bring into this moment through thought that causes us to feel unhappy and discontent with life. Memories are some of the most common thoughts that rob our happiness, but even fantasies of the future do this, simply because they take us out of the richness and aliveness of the present moment and into a made-up reality. The mind's reality is a two-dimensional reality; it doesn't have the fullness, realness, aliveness, or depth of reality, and it never will, no matter how engrossed in a fantasy we become.

Happiness is not found in thinking, as fun as thinking can be sometimes. Absorption in thoughts about the past and the future and about ourselves is not really fun. We feel compelled to think about ourselves, our past, and our future, but just notice how contracted and tense these thoughts make you feel. Such thinking doesn't result in happiness, but confusion, worry, fear, stress, and discontentment.

Forgiving and forgetting the past allows us to stay in the present moment, to drop the memories and attempts at fixing the past or being right and just be here right now and see what life is offering now in this moment. Once you allow yourself to really experience the present moment, you discover that it has everything you have ever wanted. It has the peace, happiness, contentment, and even excitement that you long for. When we are in the moment, we experience the excitement and adventure of not knowing what is coming next, and we also experience the joy our Being feels in being alive and existing in this amazing universe. When you come into the present moment, you come into contact with the real you, with your Being, which is in love with life and enjoying it all!

91: ALL YOU NEED IS LOVE

We have everything we need because all we need is love, and everyone has an unlimited supply of that. Not everyone may feel love, but it is always there and available to give to others. The way we experience the unlimited supply of love is by giving it away. That is counter-intuitive, which is why it may seem like there isn't enough love. When we believe we need to get love from outside ourselves, that sense of lack stops the love flowing from inside us to others. Believing that you need love becomes a self-fulfilling prophesy: You believe you need love because you aren't experiencing it, and in trying to get it, you fail to give it, so you don't experience it. You can't really do two things at once: If you are relating to someone, you are either giving your attention (love) to that person or trying to get something from that person. You are either in Essence (giving attention) or in ego (trying to get attention). These are very different states of consciousness, and they result in very different experiences.

The experience of the ego is one of lack. It never has enough of anything, including love. So the ego looks outside itself to get what it lacks. It tries to manipulate the world to fill its desires and so-called needs. The experience of Essence, on the other hand, is an experience of fullness. If Essence has a need, it would be to give love, to attend fully to whatever is happening right now in the present moment. Essence loves whatever is arising and gives its attention to that out of love for it. When we do that as well, we drop into Essence and fall in love with life, which is how Essence feels about life. And when we are in love with life and with the present moment, there is a natural movement outward to give to or support whatever is showing up in life.

That flow of love and attention toward life is the experience of love that everyone is looking for. It is always possible to give attention and love to whatever is showing up in our life. It is a simple choice, but not so easy to do. The ego doesn't value doing that. It doesn't believe that doing that will get it what it wants.

The irony is that giving love and attention to whatever is showing up in our life is exactly what gets us what we want, and doing what the ego thinks will make it happy results in the opposite. Life is a little like Alice's experience in Wonderland: Everything is backwards. However, once you realize that secret about life, your experience of the world changes. Life becomes bountiful and supportive rather than lacking and unkind. The kindness that flows from you creates a kind world, not only for you, but also for others. All you need is love—and you already have plenty of that to give!

92: TRYING TO BE SOMEBODY

Trying to be somebody is exhausting! (Don't we all know?) Trying to be somebody or get somewhere is a place of stress, a place of lack, an assumption that we don't already have what we need to be happy or even just okay. We all have ideas about who we are: "I'm somebody who likes this and not that, who can do this and not that, who does this and not that, who had this happen and not that, who wants this and not that...." And that somebody invariably feels lacking in some way. However that somebody doesn't actually exist, except as ideas about ourselves. We all have a storyline going on in our minds about who we are, where we've come from, where we want to go, and what we need to get there.

Often the past is something we feel needs to be redeemed by the future: Something happened or didn't happen in the past, so we feel we need something to happen to make us feel better about our past, our life, and ourselves! Without a sense of something being wrong or lacking, we wouldn't need the future to be a certain way so that we, once and for all, could feel like we are okay and our life is okay just the way it is.

The storyline in our minds is usually a rather unhappy one, but we hope it will have a happy ending. If it doesn't, that will prove that we were right all along—we are unworthy! And we will never be happy. The mind usually focuses on some goal or desire that it believes will redeem us, something we don't currently have: "When I finally meet the right person, when I have a baby, when I'm free to travel around the world, when I have enough money, when I lose weight.... then I will be happy. Then I will be whole."

The egoic mind plays a terrible trick on us in telling us we are flawed and that we have to do something or get something to be happy or acceptable (To others? To ourselves? To God? To whom?). This is the most basic lie, and it underlies our humanity. It is the Original Sin we each seem to carry around with us: "I'm bad and imperfect, so I have to do or get something to be better, make amends, or right the situation." Some version of this story runs through everyone's mind or unconscious. Within humanity, a sense of unworthiness runs deep. What we do to soothe, heal, or fill this lack varies greatly, but most of us feel a need to do or get something.

So much of our doing and striving is fueled by this sense of lack. What if you just stopped for a moment and took a good look at the truth: There's nothing missing within you or about life. Life is and you are just as life is and you are meant to be—because life is and you are! Who knows why? We don't know why things are the way they are, but to assume they should be otherwise is to make a monumental mistake, one leads to a lot of suffering.

Things are as they are, we are as we are, others are as they are— and things are constantly changing. Why should anything be different than it is in this moment? Just because the ego wants it to be different? What is the ego? The ego is the originator of the thought "I want...." The ego doesn't exist except as thoughts and desires. Where did all our thoughts and desires come from? Now, that is the great mystery.

Our thoughts and desires are the programming that makes us human, and part of this programming is a sense of lack and a drive to fill that sense of lack. This makes the world go around, but you don't need this sense of lack to make your world go around. It would be quite a different world if lack and desire weren't running it. The sense of lack and the desire to fill it, to be whole, to be special, to be somebody, holds the ego in place. It gives it a self-image and something to do. Without a self-image as flawed and the desire to be somebody, who would you be? The ego is nothing without its images and goals, and that's the truth.

When you just stop trying for a moment and look and see what is really here, all you can find is consciousness experiencing life. Consciousness doesn't look a certain way, it doesn't have a name, and it isn't trying to be somebody or get somewhere. It's just enjoying life just as it is. That which is capable of noticing the *you* that is trying to be somebody is who you really are.

You can drop out of the race to be somebody and get it right anytime you like. You only have to see that what is discontent and striving to be happy is just the *you* that's part of the story of you, not the real you. The *you* in the story you create about yourself is striving very hard to be okay and be happy, but that isn't who you really are! You are that which is outside that story. Whenever you realize this and allow yourself to just experience life, free of the *me* who is having a particular experience that it likes or doesn't like, you drop out of that story.

93: HOW TO GET MORE LOVE IN YOUR LIFE

The question, "How can I get more love in my life?" is itself part of the problem, because this question assumes that you don't have enough love right now and that you have to do something to get it. It also assumes that love is something we get from other people. If you believe these assumptions, you will get busy trying to do something to get love, and you will be doing those things from a sense of lack, which is not particularly attractive. When we believe we lack love, we create a sense of lack within ourselves, and that sense of lack becomes somewhat of a self-fulfilling prophesy, as people sense that we want something from them.

When we are looking to get something from people, even love, it's coming from the ego, which is a place of self-centeredness, tension, and discontentment: "What can you do for me?" Other egos are also looking for what someone else can do for them. Those who are looking for something or someone to fulfill them from the outside aren't likely to find it, not only because other people don't necessarily want to fill that role, but also, more importantly, because we can never get enough love from outside ourselves to fulfill the ego's sense of lack.

The only solution to wanting more love is realizing the truth about love: It is our nature to love, and each of us has an unlimited supply of it, but we must choose to activate this supply of love by giving it away. The way to have the experience of love is to give love. When love is flowing from us, we experience love. It doesn't come from others. This becomes apparent when someone is in love with us, but we aren't in love with him or her. Someone loving us isn't enough to get us to feel love. Love isn't something someone can give us. What we really want is to feel the love that we *are*. The source of love is inside of us, and we experience love when we choose to give it to others.

We are used to thinking of love as an emotion, a feeling that sweeps over us, like when we fall in love. Falling in love is the most wonderful feeling, and yet, the feeling of falling in love isn't true love, and it doesn't last. We long for that feeling to be our ongoing experience, but it can't be. Falling in love is a feeling that comes and eventually goes. True love is not so much a feeling as a way of being. It's a state of acceptance, openness, kindness, and receptivity to another. We experience love as a result of being open and attentive to and accepting of whomever is in front of us.

Love also flows when we are simply open to and accepting of life and whatever experience we are having. Love flows from us (and is experienced by us) whenever we are fully present and accepting of how life is showing up, whether a relationship is part of that moment or not. Love flows whenever we aren't complaining about life, wanting something different, or judging and evaluating whatever is going on.

Love is our natural state. It's the state we drop into whenever we are simply saying yes to how life is showing up in the moment. The only thing that can interfere with this yes is the mind saying no to life. So the only thing that can interfere with love is a thought! No person or circumstance can interfere with our ability to feel love unless we allow it to. And no person can make us feel love unless we allow it either. The really good news is that love is a possibility in every moment. It's in our control. It's our choice: We can choose to love whatever and whomever we are experiencing or not.

Our default position as humans seems to be to reject and find fault with our experience and with the people we encounter. But that doesn't have to be our response to life. We have the power to ignore the judgments and negativity of our minds and to open our hearts in acceptance to whatever happens to be showing up. When we do that, we discover that there's no shortage of love. When we are very present to whatever experience we are having instead of involved in our thoughts about life, love flows outward from within us to whatever and whomever we are experiencing. We also find that love from others is the natural response to this outward flow. But the love that's returned to us is not the source of our love, as nice as that love might be.

You are the source of love, and you have the power to feel love. In any moment, you can choose love instead of following your train of thoughts about what you want and how you'd like things to be. You are the creator of your experience because you can choose how you respond to life. We may not be able to control what comes our way and whether we are in a relationship with someone at a particular time. But we can control how we choose to see and respond to whatever life brings us. Once we've learned that we are masters of our experience in this way, life can be full of love whether we have someone special returning our love or not.

94: BECOME AWARE OF "I" THOUGHTS

The thoughts that involve "I" usually cause some level of suffering. Notice the types of thoughts the word "I" is involved in: "I don't like...." "I never...." "I always...." "I can't...." Occasionally, thoughts with "I" or "me" in them are functional, neutral, and benign. But more often a story about the *me* follows "I," and that story often depicts some shortcoming or problem that needs to be solved. These stories and "problems" are the ego's spin on ourselves and life. They are how the ego defines us and life. They are a small story that can never encompass the whole truth about ourselves and life. And they are usually a negative story, one that makes us feel bad.

If you don't like the ego's stories or definition or if they make you feel bad, you don't have to take them on as yours. They are your ego's stories and definitions, but they are not yours. You get to choose the stories you tell about yourself, others, and life. You get to define yourself. This is a very empowering realization: You are the master of your self-image! If you don't take mastery over it, the ego will continue to define you and tell its stories of woe and negativity. And you will live out those definitions and stories unconsciously.

The truth is, you don't even need a self-image to exist and function. Self-images are created by the ego and are, in fact, what make up the ego. If you don't like your self-image, then create a different one, or better yet, move beyond all self-images and other mental constructs. You don't need ideas about yourself or others to be alive, to be happy, and to function beautifully in this world. Your self-images have often limited you and interfered with your happiness, so why buy into them and maintain them?

We have self-images and believe them because we are given them, in a sense. They are our programming, and they will define us and affect our experience of life for as long as we are unconscious of them. Once we become conscious of our self-images, we can become free of them or create ones that are truer, ones that are more aligned with our true nature. Once we do that, we can live from a different place, a freer, kinder, happier place because our true nature is happy, loving, and content.

If you want to be happy, loving, and content, discover the thoughts that keep you from feeling happy, loving, content, and at peace with life. See through them—see their falseness and say no to them. Say no to the mental reality the ego attempts to create. You really don't have to live in that world once you become more conscious of your "I" thoughts, where those thoughts come from (the ego—your programming), how they limit you—and how untrue they are. That is halfway to freedom. The other half is recognizing who you really are, which is possible once the mind is quiet. So first recognize who you are *not*, and then it's much easier to recognize who you really are. This is the essence of the spiritual path—discovering the false with us and uncovering our true nature.

95: THE TRUTH ABOUT RESPONSIBILITY

This may sound sacrilegious to you, but I will state it anyway: You are not responsible for other people. How can you be? You cannot control other people's choices, including how they choose to see something, so how can you be responsible? This may be obvious in regard to strangers, but many of us, especially those who are parents, have difficulty not feeling responsible for our loved ones' choices and happiness. As much as we would like to be able to protect others and help them to be happy and make the right choices, we are not that powerful. We can't make anyone do or feel anything. That is in their power, and their power alone.

Accepting this reality is difficult, especially for parents; and yet, to not accept it is often to suffer needlessly. Not accepting that we can't control other people's happiness and choices leads to suffering, and this suffering doesn't serve anyone, neither the person who's suffering nor the person being suffered over. The trouble with suffering is it keeps us tied to the ego and its perceptions about life, which tend to be negative and fear-based.

We want to be able to control other people and their choices because we are afraid for them and because we don't trust life. We are afraid of what will happen to them on their own, without our help. Essentially, we don't trust them to choose well or that they will learn from their choices, and we don't trust life to teach them and evolve them.

As parents, we feel responsible for teaching our children, and we think that if we teach them well, they should be able to avoid being unhappy, making mistakes, and having problems. But how can that be true? No one on this planet has ever not been unhappy, not made mistakes, and not had problems. We have to be willing to let our children and other people live their lives, make their choices, and learn and grow from them—just as we have.

The mistakes and problems in life aren't wrong, which is how the ego sees things, but part of the design of life in this realm, where we learn and evolve as a result of such challenges. Mistakes and problems are a natural part of life. Even the suffering that comes from them is natural and serves a purpose in our evolution. Eventually, we discover that suffering is actually unnecessary and doesn't have to accompany mistakes and problems.

The fact that we can only help others so much must be obvious, but the ego still often argues with this fact and takes it personally when we aren't able to help someone. The best that we as a parent, teacher, or other guide or counselor can do is provide information, love, support, and an environment that offers what someone needs. The rest—what someone does or doesn't do with what is offered—is out of our hands.

We aren't responsible for other people's choices or their experience, not even their experience of us. How can we be, since we can't choose for them and we can't determine their thoughts, feelings, and attitudes? Other people are in charge of their own choices and inner experience. People create their experience of something by what they tell themselves about it, and of course, we create our own experience of life the same way.

This discovery is actually a great relief, because it means we are in control of our own happiness and our own experience of life. One of the best gifts you can give someone is this great truth: You are the one responsible for your own happiness, not anyone or anything else. This understanding empowers us to choose love rather than hatred, to be happy rather than unhappy, to be grateful rather than to complain, to grow rather than not grow, to love what is rather than focus on what isn't.

This understanding is a very helpful one. And yet, we still aren't in control of whether someone accepts and lives this truth or not after offering it to them. We have to leave that up to that person and to life to continue to show that person what he or she needs to learn. Life is a trustworthy teacher. We all eventually learn to navigate life wisely and happily, although doing so may take many, many lifetimes. Wisdom is available all around us, but like taking a horse to water, we can't make someone drink from the well of wisdom. If they don't, it's not our business, but their business and life's business. So, we must leave it up to them and up to life. We must let go and let God, as they say. Fortunately, what we let go to, call it God or whatever you will, is good and trustworthy.

96: AWAKENING

Every moment is an opportunity to be awake. Awakeness, or Essence, is available whenever we are simply present to all of what *is* instead of the small slice of life that is thoughts and feelings. Whenever we drop out of identification with the commentator in our head, we land in the present and experience being awake. Awakeness is who you really are! You can't *not* be awake if you are alive! What is it that is aware of reading these words? That Awakeness—Awareness—is who you really are.

Awakeness is obscured by identifying with the egoic mind, which pretends to be who you are. But Awakeness is ever-present and experienced whenever we give our attention to it instead of to our egoic mind and all of its thoughts about *me*. Everyone experiences Awakeness many times in every day. Whenever you feel peaceful, content, and happy, however briefly, you are experiencing it. Most people don't experience it for very long because their mind recaptures their attention, but anyone can increase the amount of time they stay in Awakeness through meditation and other spiritual practices.

Awakening happens when our identity permanently shifts from being primarily identified with the ego to being primarily identified with Essence. For many, it happens at a particular moment in time, which forever changes how they relate to life. The experience of this shift may be very dramatic—mind-blowing, as they say—or quite quiet and simple. It's different for everyone.

After awakening, ego identification may still happen occasionally because the ego often attempts to reconstitute and regain control, and any unhealed conditioning may still have the power to draw us into ego identification. But that's all part of the healing process. From Awakeness, conditioning can be healed by seeing it, inquiring into it, and allowing and accepting it. Eventually much, if not all, of our conditioning will stop arising.

Many find that the structures of their life change after awakening, although that may not be necessary if those structures already serve Essence. To function fully as Essence, a lifestyle that supports it is required. You can't necessarily expect to live the same life that people who are ego-driven live and remain fully awake. A certain commitment to Essence is needed to keep from falling into a semi-sleep, where you begin to suffer again. Without such a commitment, those who've seen the truth but aren't seated in it firmly enough may get pulled back into their conditioning and old egoic ways of being.

Very few people drop the ego altogether and are never bothered by it again. This is so rare, but the fact that it does occur is very confusing to the many who still experience the presence of an ego after awakening. For most, the experience after awakening is that the egoic mind still chatters away and identification can still happen, but none of it is a problem. You know the mind isn't who you are, so you don't listen to it. And you know that your conditioning isn't *yours*, so you let it be there and let it show you what you need to understand about it in order to heal it.

Awakening is the culmination of all of our lifetimes on earth, but it is really only the beginning of a much longer journey of service to this dimension and, ultimately, to every dimension beyond.

97: WANTING TO AWAKEN

When it's time to awaken, a longing for awakening arises from deep within us. This longing comes from Essence and spurs on our spiritual growth. However, it is often co-opted by the ego, which sees awakening as an opportunity to be special, feel good, get what it wants, or escape life. When the desire to awaken is co-opted by the ego, the result is suffering, as with every other desire the ego has. To the ego, how we are and how life is right now never seems good enough but flawed and lacking the ingredients for happiness. This is the ego's constant state, a state of discontentment.

Many suffer greatly over wanting to awaken, as over every other desire. That's because desire by its nature takes us out of the moment, where contentment is possible, and into a dream of something better in the future, which creates an experience in this moment of lack and, therefore, dissatisfaction.

It's natural to want to escape this state of dissatisfaction, and that drives us along the spiritual path toward awakening. Suffering does eventually wake everybody up. But what we may not realize when we are ego identified is that our discontentment is caused by longing for something else—for spiritual awakening or whatever else is desired—not by the actual absence of anything. There's so much to be grateful for right now, but the ego doesn't see this. When we are able to acknowledge what we are grateful for about our current circumstances, we drop out of the ego and into Essence and experience contentment—awakeness.

The good news is that you don't have to have a spiritual awakening to experience awakeness. If you want to experience what it's like to be awakened, just be here right now and not in your thoughts about what's happening now, the past, the future, or what you want. Just be here right now. Do you want awakening enough to turn away from your thoughts about yourself and from your desires, which are just more thoughts? That's all that is required, really. Do you want awakening enough to just be present in this moment without all of your thoughts?

The ego doesn't want to be present, and it doesn't want to give up thoughts about *me* because then it would no longer exist, since it exists only as thoughts about *me*. The *you* that you think of yourself as and all the desires that go with that are just thoughts about you. What is really alive and living this life isn't a thought, but a Being, while the thoughts about you are the self you pretend to be—a masterful, but false, disguise for this Being.

When, for even a moment, you stop thinking this *you* into existence by being involved with stories and self-images of yourself and, instead, experience the Being that you are, you are awake. When you live from this place, it's said that you are awakened. But isn't it wonderful that, in any moment, you can choose to experience awakeness by simply disregarding and not identifying with thoughts about yourself and with the desires of the ego?

The process of awakening is a process of learning to disidentify with the egoic mind, or the false self, and identify instead with the Being that you are, who is here right now and always has been— looking out of your eyes, breathing, and moving your body. Who else would be doing these things? The *you* that you think you are stops existing as soon as you stop thinking, so how can that be who you are? The false self, or ego, comes and goes with thoughts about *me*, *my* life, and what *I* want. When you are involved with thoughts about *me*, then you exist as this *you*, and when you aren't, you exist as Beingness.

The process of awakening is facilitated by meditation because meditation trains us to detach from the egoic mind, or false self, and experience Being, or Essence. The more we meditate, the easier it becomes to detach from the egoic mind in our daily life and express our Being. So, do you want to awaken enough to make time to meditate? The ego doesn't want to meditate, so you may have to overcome the ego's resistance to it because, naturally, it doesn't want to disappear, which is what happens in meditation.

The longing to awaken motivates us to do things that support awakening. It drives us to attend spiritual gatherings, read spiritual books, meditate, question, inquire, do healing work, be quiet, and just be. This longing is a force that calls us Home, but you have to be willing to answer its call. When you do, it feels fulfilling. The egoic mind, however, might tell you that you don't have time for these things or that they aren't enough or aren't making a difference or are too difficult or that the teacher is flawed. It will try to interfere with the natural process of awakening. It's good to be aware of how the ego tries to hinder this process, while at the same time, enflaming your desire to awaken in a way that causes you to suffer.

There's no need to suffer over awakening because each of us is waking up in exactly the way and at exactly the time that is best for us. And you especially don't have to suffer when you realize that in this very moment you have the capacity to experience awakeness simply by choosing to be here now in this moment without involvement in the story of *me*. Do you want to awaken enough to choose being awake in the moment to being lost in the dream of *me*?

98: SUFFERING OVER SUFFERING

People suffer tremendously over the fact that they are suffering, especially when the goal of the spiritual search is to end all suffering. Then, not suffering becomes just one more failed goal for the ego to suffer over. Resisting our suffering can cause more suffering or just as much as resisting whatever else we are resisting about our life, which caused the suffering in the first place. Being upset because we are suffering holds the initial suffering in place and prolongs it. Once we have seen this, there is the possibility of just allowing the suffering we are experiencing to be here, for now. If it's here, then let it be here. That acceptance provides an environment where the contraction we are feeling can begin to relax.

No one can suffer interminably; it's too exhausting. We can only suffer so long before our consciousness expands again and we see things from a bigger perspective. Suffering is caused by seeing things from a very small perspective, the ego's perspective. This small perspective makes us feel contracted, small, and powerless. But we can only identify with that false perspective and the false self so long before who we really are shines again and overshadows the false self. Often just out of sheer exhaustion, we drop back into Essence. What a relief it is to no longer be holding such a small perspective! It's very tiring to be contracted, tense, and upset.

When we finally let go of the small perspective—the ego's lie, limited story, or belief—we relax into just being, which is inherently pleasant, relaxed, peaceful, accepting—mellow. The only thing that can cause us to contract and feel tense again is believing something else the mind is telling us that doesn't represent the complete truth about life or our situation. Have you noticed what negative stories the mind tells you? The ego puts a negative spin on life, which stirs up negative feelings if we believe those stories. That's the ego's purpose, but we don't have to buy into its version of life.

The good news is that every time you contract, you can be sure you will expand! Suffering isn't a problem because it isn't forever—and it isn't fatal! Of course, no one likes to suffer, but it does come and go, like everything else in life. Suffering is a bit like the weather: Storms blow in and then dissipate. No matter how intensely we are suffering, it will run its course.

It's possible to not suffer, or at least not so much. Suffering is unnecessary. And yet very few people are entirely free of suffering. It's rare and therefore perhaps unrealistic to expect to be entirely free of suffering in this lifetime. How wonderful it is if you can reduce the amount you suffer even a little! If you can, you can be sure the amount you suffer will continue to decrease as you get better at turning away from the egoic mind and staying in the present moment.

Being present in the moment takes practice, like everything else. You practice listening to the egoic mind all the time, so it's going to take practice to learn to not listen to it. When you feel impatient with your progress, remind yourself that impatience comes from the ego. It creates the problem and then suffers over it. Suffering over our suffering is just more ego, and all you have to do is just see that. And be gentle with yourself. It's really hard being human. If it were easy to wake up out of the ego and never suffer again, there would be many more people having that experience!

The funny thing is that as soon as we accept our suffering, and suffering over our suffering, we have taken a step back from the ego and dropped into Essence, where the mistaken beliefs that caused the suffering can be seen through and healed. The more we are able to see that the beliefs that caused our suffering are untrue, the sooner we will be free of the suffering caused by them. Suffering gives us the opportunity to see our conditioning, see its falseness, and become free of it. Suffering isn't so bad! It's actually intended to set us free from the egoic mind, and eventually that's exactly what it does. Because suffering is unpleasant, we learn to question what we are thinking, especially when spiritual teachings encourage such inquiry.

The spiritual technologies and spiritual understanding exist that can free us from much suffering, but please don't suffer if you are still suffering sometimes! There's no hurry to become free. When suffering is no longer seen as a problem, then it can come and go. When suffering shows up, it's an opportunity to see through any mistaken beliefs and negativity. Where's the problem in that?

Contraction and expansion of consciousness is part of life as long as we are human. Whether you suffer over contraction or not depends on how much acceptance you bring to it when it's happening and how much compassion and tenderness you give yourself for being human. The solution to suffering is acceptance, compassion, gentleness, and love for yourself and others who happen to be believing the ego's stories.

99: THE HUMAN DRAMA

Thoughts show up in our mind from who knows where, and we assume they belong to us. We assume they are what we think, what we believe, what we should do, and what we are. What if your thoughts are just the conditioning you were given, and they are no more yours and no more true than someone else's thoughts, which are no more theirs and no more true than yours? Your thoughts are just part of the programming that makes you human, while you are actually a spiritual being.

Like the color of your eyes or your personality, your thoughts were just given to you, and they make up the character that you think you are. But are you that human character? Or are you what is reading these words and contemplating whether or not you are that character? Can you be that character *and* be what is aware of and what contemplates that character? How is that possible? Maybe you are something beyond that character, but you are pretending to be that character. That would explain it, wouldn't it? Every so often, we have glimpses of the Actor behind that character, glimpses of what is playing at being *you.*

Just as an actor has a choice to continue acting or to do something else, once we have realized we are the Actor, we have a choice to continue acting out the drama of this character or not. When the play is over, the actor goes home. Likewise, when we are done with the drama of the character we are playing, we come Home. You retire from being *you* and give up the trappings of that character—the desires, beliefs, opinions, fears, fantasies, judgments, self-images, and other conditioning—and relax into your true self, which was hidden behind the costume all along.

Once you have retired from being that character, life continues, but it continues without all the drama and pain. It turns out that the conditioning caused the drama and suffering, not life, because when the trappings are shed, so is the suffering. What a surprise! You really were just pretending to be someone. It felt like you were someone who was opposed to life and struggling to find contentment, but all you needed to do was shed the trappings, the conditioning, that made you that character. The curtain goes down on the experience of being that character, but life continues, as Essence expresses itself through you more purely now. How happy and content Essence is with life, and what a relief it is to be free of the stories and the drama!

ABOUT THE AUTHOR

Gina Lake is a spiritual teacher and the author of numerous books about awakening to one's true nature, including *Trusting Life, Embracing the Now, Radical Happiness, Living in the Now, Return to Essence, Loving in the Moment, What About Now? Anatomy of Desire,* and *Getting Free.* She is also a gifted intuitive with a master's degree in counseling psychology and over twenty years experience supporting people in their spiritual growth. Her website offers information about her books, free e-books, book excerpts, a monthly newsletter, a blog, and audio and video recordings:

www.radicalhappiness.com

Books by Gina Lake

(Available in paperback, Kindle, and other e-book formats.)

Embracing the Now: Finding Peace and Happiness in What Is.
The Now—this moment—is the true source of happiness and peace
and the key to living a fulfilled and meaningful life. *Embracing the
Now* is a collection of essays that can serve as daily reminders of the
deepest truths. Full of clear insight and wisdom, *Embracing the Now*
explains how the mind keeps us from being in the moment, how to
move into the Now and stay there, and what living from the Now is
like. It also explains how to overcome stumbling blocks to being in
the Now, such as fears, doubts, misunderstandings, judgments,
distrust of life, desires, and other conditioned ideas that are behind
human suffering.

Radical Happiness: A Guide to Awakening provides the keys to
experiencing the happiness that is ever-present and not dependent
on circumstances. This happiness doesn't come from getting what
you want, but from wanting what is here now. It comes from
realizing that who you think you are is not who you really are. This
is a radical perspective! *Radical Happiness* describes the nature of
the egoic state of consciousness and how it interferes with
happiness, what awakening and enlightenment are, and how to live
in the world after awakening.

***Trusting Life: Overcoming the Fear and Beliefs That Block Peace
and Happiness.*** Fear and distrust keep us from living the life we
were meant to live, and they are the greatest hurdles to seeing the
truth about life—that it is good, abundant, supportive, and
potentially joyous. *Trusting Life* is a deep exploration into the
mystery of who we are, why we suffer, why we don't trust life, and
how to become more trusting. It offers evidence that life is
trustworthy and tools for overcoming the fear and beliefs that keep
us from falling in love with life.

***Loving in the Moment: Moving from Ego to Essence in
Relationships.*** Having a truly meaningful relationship requires
choosing love over your conditioning, that is, your ideas, fantasies,
desires, images, and beliefs. *Loving in the Moment* describes how to
move beyond conditioning, judgment, anger, romantic illusions,
and differences to the experience of love and Oneness with
another. It explains how to drop into the core of your Being, where
Oneness and love exist, and be with others from there.

***Anatomy of Desire: How to Be Happy Even When You Don't
Get What You Want*** will help you discriminate between your
Heart's desires and the ego's and to relate to the ego's desires in a
way that reduces suffering and increases joy. By pointing out the
myths about desire that keep us tied to our ego's desires and the
suffering they cause, *Anatomy of Desire* will help you be happy
regardless of your desires and whether you are attaining them. So it
is also about spiritual freedom, or liberation, which comes from
following the Heart, our deepest desires, instead of the ego's
desires. It is about becoming a lover of life rather than a desirer.

Return to Essence: How to Be in the Flow and Fulfill Your Life's Purpose describes how to get into the flow and stay there and how to live life from there. Being in the flow and not being in the flow are two very different states. One is dominated by the ego-driven mind, which is the cause of suffering, while the other is the domain of Essence, the Divine within each of us. You are meant to live in the flow. The flow is the experience of Essence—your true self—as it lives life through you and fulfills its purpose for this life.

Living in the Now: How to Live as the Spiritual Being That You Are. The 99 essays in *Living in the Now* will help you realize your true nature and live as that. They answer many question raised by the spiritual search and offer wisdom on subjects such as fear, anger, happiness, aging, boredom, desire, patience, faith, forgiveness, acceptance, love, commitment, hope, purpose, meaning, meditation, being present, emotions, trusting life, trusting your Heart, and many other deep subjects. These essays will help you become more conscious, present, happy, loving, grateful, at peace, and fulfilled. Each essay stands on its own and can be used for daily contemplation.

Getting Free: How to Move Beyond Conditioning and Be Happy. Freedom from your conditioning is possible, but the mind is a formidable opponent to freedom. To be free requires a new way of thinking or, rather, not thinking. To a large extent, healing our conditioning involves changing our relationship to our mind and discovering who we really are. *Getting Free* will help you do that. It will also help you reprogram your mind; clear negative thoughts and self-images; use meditation, prayer, forgiveness, and gratitude; work with spiritual forces to assist healing and clear negativity; and heal entrenched issues from the past.

What About Now? Reminders for Being in the Moment. The secret to happiness is moving out of the mind and learning to delight in each moment. In *What About Now*, you will find over 150 quotes from Gina Lake's books—*Radical Happiness, Embracing the Now, Loving in the Moment, Living in the Now*, and others—that will inspire and enable you to be more present. These empowering quotes will wake you up out of your ordinary consciousness and help you live with more love, contentment, gratitude, and awe.

For more info, please visit the "Books" page at
http://www.radicalhappiness.com

133.9 LAK
Lake, Gina.
Living in the now

14153670R00150

Made in the USA
Charleston, SC
24 August 2012

THIS BIRD
HAS FLOWN